Marketing the Marketers

50 Ways Marketing Services Providers Can Woo and Win New Clients

HENRY DEVRIES

authorHOUSE®

AuthorHouse™
1663 Liberty Drive, Suite 200
Bloomington, IN 47403
www.authorhouse.com
Phone: 1-800-839-8640

First published by AuthorHouse 3/9/2009

ISBN: 978-1-4389-5772-2 (sc)

Printed in the United States of America
Bloomington, Indiana

This book is printed on acid-free paper.

Contents

Acknowledgements

This is what I like to think about and thank about. I would like to thank my creator, my parents, my sisters, my children, my mentors, my clients, my students, my colleagues and my mastermind for all they have given me. My blessings include a positive mental attitude, sound physical health, harmony in human relationships, freedom from fear, hope of future achievement, faith in my creator, a willingness to share abundance with others, a labor of love, an open mind on all subjects, knowledge of how to have self discipline, insights on how to understand people and financial security through the knowledge of how to create a business that serves the wants of others.

May all who read this have cash flow and time to enjoy it.

CHAPTER 1: WHO ELSE WANTS TO TURN CLIENT PAIN INTO MARKETING GAIN?

If you are a marketer who is a little frustrated about how to attract enough clients, you are not alone. Many marketing communications consultants – advertising agencies, public relations firms, interactive Internet/Web companies, and graphic design studios -- struggle with marketing and hope that networking will bring them enough clients. This isn't exactly hoping and wishing for clients, but it is darn close.

There is a better way to get marketing communications clients. First you probe for pain, then you educate prospects how to solve their pains in general. The more you educate how to solve their pain in general the more that will hire you for specific services.

Unfortunately, many marketing services firms who learn this truth find the idea of writing and speaking about client pain too daunting and even mysterious. Most feel this is only for a select few mega-minds like David Ogilvy, Peter Drucker or Tom Peters, but that is a miscalculated view. You don't need to write three dozen books and have them translated into 30 languages. Just becoming a local marketing guru can work wonders.

Understanding the psychology of clients provides critical evidence of the validity of the speak up and get published approach. Consulting is what economists sometimes call "credence" goods, in that purchasers must place great faith in those who sell the services. How can potential clients trust you if they never hear what you have to say?

The good news is there exists a body of knowledge that some have discovered to grow their consultants. As an example, management consulting firms like McKinsey & Co. pioneered the approach beginning in the 1940s and now have it down to a science. Ad agencies like Ogilvy and Mather refined the art. We have named it the Educating Expert Model for finding clients.

How do you get started as a marketing communications guru? First, understand that generating new clients is an investment and should be measured like any other investment. Next, quit wasting money on ineffective means — don't stone me before hearing me out — like brochures, advertising and sponsorships. Rather than creating a brochure, start by writing how-to articles. Those articles turn into speeches and seminars. The best marketing investment you can make is to get help creating informative Web sites, hosting persuasive seminars, booking speaking engagements, and getting published as a newsletter columnist and eventually a book author.

Please know this: the universe rewards activity. Start by being curious and asking clients about their pains. Gather information on how to solve those worries, frustrations and concerns. Be the expert who educates people on how they compare to their peers and the best ways to overcome their obstacles. The more prospects you inform how to solve their problems in general, the more will hire you for the specifics.

CHAPTER 2: ARE YOU INTO PAIN?

Did you know that psychologists and sociologists have repeatedly found that people are more motivated to avoid pain than to seek pleasure?

Your target market experiences its own unique frustrations and pains. The secret to maximizing your attraction factor is to articulate the worries, frustrations and concerns that you solve. As the old adage states, "People don't care what you know, until they know that you care." Truly identifying your market's predicament tells them that you understand and empathize with them.

The Pain-Into-Gain Riddle

How will clients hire you unless they trust you?

How, in turn, will they trust ideas they have not heard?

How, in turn, will they hear without someone to speak?

How, in turn, will you speak unless you have a solution?

How, in turn, will you have a solution unless you understand their pain?

How will you understand their pain unless you listen?

If you are a marketer who struggles with marketing, you are not alone. Many marketing communications consultants are tired of the rejection, frustration and mystery of marketing.

There is a better way to attract clients. The secret is to turn their pain into your gain. Start by asking clients about their pains. Then gather information on how to solve those worries, frustrations and concerns.

Let us ask you this (now be honest): Do you really understand the problems of your prospects and clients? Or do you just think you know? Make no doubt about it, the stakes are high. Wrong marketing messages will cost you potential clients and lead to more struggles and frustration.

So here's how to become a new client magnet. Each group of prospects experiences its own unique frustrations and pains. What's the secret to crafting a marketing message that will maximize your attraction factor? Ask them (or have someone ask for you) about their pains. Start by asking a sample about their ideal business, and them segue into problems. Listen carefully to the exact words they use (you will want to mimic them in your marketing messages).

When you interview some current, past and potential clients about the pains you solve, here are 10 questions you should always ask:

1. Describe for me the "ideal" experience with a _____ (your profession or line of consulting). How do most compare to this ideal?

2. Describe for me a recent time that the experience was less than ideal.

3. What are the three most important aspects of doing business with a_____.

4. If I said a _____ was a good value, what would that mean to you?

5. In what ways does dealing with a _____ cost you besides money (time, hassle, effort, etc.)?

6. What is the biggest pain about working with a _____.

7. Would you recommend a _____ to a friend or colleague? Why, or why not?

8. How does working with a _____ help you make money?

9. What does a _____ do really well?

10. If you had the opportunity to work with a _____ again, would you?

    Why, or why not?

CHAPTER 3: HOW TO BE PAID TO MARKET

Would you like to add $100,000 or more to your annual income? Read on.

One day I was taking my two teenage sons from our home in San Diego to Disneyland. Along the way I stopped to give a speech to a group of Orange County business owners while the boys munched on a fast food breakfast in the car. While that speech generated five figures worth of revenue for me as I picked up various paid speeches and consulting work as a result of my talk, the speaking fee was a few hundred dollars. As I came back to the car I tucked my honorarium check (more honor than rarium) in the glove compartment. My older son asked about the check and I told him these business owners actually paid me to market my services to them. "Sweet," said my son, "that is the perfect crime."

The Five Ways To Get Paid To Market

Here are some more examples of this perfect crime, committed by coaching clients I am especially proud of. A marketing research consultant I coached complained that he wasn't getting any consulting business for the past six months from a Fortune 500 client. There are more ways to get paid than straight consulting, I told him. Often companies that don't have money for consultants have money in their training budgets. So he organized a seminar, held the event near the company's headquarters and sold 11 seats for $600 a piece to that same Fortune 500 client. After the event several attendees found some budget and he landed about $75,000 in marketing research consulting projects. Later he charged another client $1,500 (he is worth much more) for a 90-minute talk at a company meeting that will net him consulting contracts in the five figures.

A public relations firm owner I coached was able to double her revenue in a year (we're talking over $100,000 more) just by having different conversations about her pricing with potential clients. Actually, when she raised her rates, it was a signal to the business community that she was in demand and a hot commodity. But alas, how to make even more money. She soon realized there are only so many hours in a week (168, to be precise) and only so much you can charge clients per hour.

To increase her revenue she needed to leverage her time. She created some self published guide books and started offering her expertise through workshops. This leverages her time and she is creating new streams of revenue.

This chapter is not for those who want to calm their nerves as they approach a podium. There will be no words of wisdom about how to conquer those common fears of public speaking (I hear Toastmasters is great for that). This is about professional speaking, not public speaking. This is for professionals and consultants who know that promoting their business with public speaking is the best way to build credibility and keep their pipeline filled with qualified prospects.

Truly, the best proactive lead generation strategy is to regularly demonstrate your expertise by giving informative and entertaining talks in front of targeted groups of potential new clients. The trick is knowing who to contact to get booked as a speaker and developing a topic that will draw the right audience.

Here are five potential perfect crimes, being paid to market your services. These are venues that write checks to consultants to speak:

1. **Keynotes and breakouts at association and trade group meetings.** A keynote is typically 30 to 90 minutes and usually focuses on a broad topic of interest to all attendees. A breakout session is one of the side sessions at a meeting and last from 45 to 90 minutes. This is the glamour field of professional speaking. Competition is fierce and the big fees go to celebrities (the group is trading on their star status to attract attendees). I put speaking at Vistage groups (formerly TEC) of about a dozen company presidents for half a day at $500 per speech in this category.

2. **Corporate training**. These are typically half-day or full-day seminars and workshops conducted for a private client, usually a corporation, for a group of its employees. This might be the most lucrative field for speaking because there are many consultants that have training budgets. Several clients who make hundreds speaking for Vistage make thousands when they deliver the same presentations to consultants. This one-two punch has made several clients an extra $100,000 per year.

3. **Sponsoring your own public seminars**. This is typically a full-day seminar or workshop where registration is open to the public. You market the event and earn a profit (or loss). This business is about putting fannies in seats. Many times it is a break even proposition getting the attendees there, and then you make your real money selling information products and consulting services at the back of the room after the event is over. Fees can range from $800 to $1,000 per day per attendee all the way down to my three-hour Lunch and Learn seminars for $25.

4. **Teaching at colleges and for public seminar consultants**. An alternative to running the seminar yourself is to find a sponsor. This might be for a company like Career Tracks or The Learning Annex. Or you might approach

the adult education marketplace through a college or university extended studies program. Typically you might earn 25 percent of what the students pay all the way up to $1,000 for a day.

5. **Speaking at fundraising workshops where you split the gate**. Another alternative to running the seminar yourself is to approach a trade group or association and offer to stage a fundraising seminar. They promote the event to their constituents and you agree to split the profits (typically 50/50 and you may or may not offer them 10 percent of any informational products like books and CDs that you sell in the back of the room after the event).

The Best Book I've Read On The Subject

If you want to read one book on the subject I recommend *Money Talks: How To Make A Million As A Speaker* by Alan Weiss, author of *Million Dollar Consulting*. The paperback book is published by McGraw-Hill and sells for $16.95. If you are really interested in the subject, I personally recommend the Odd Couple CD set Weiss sells on his Web site for $150. If you want to join the ranks of the top paid consultants, those who make $1 million a year, this is a great investment.

Bestselling author Weiss used to give speeches for free. Now his income from professional speaking and consulting totals more than $1 million a year.

Weiss is a contrarian. Many books on professional speaking say you start by coming up with a few great topics. Weiss couldn't disagree more.

"Listen carefully because few in speaking heed the following, and I'm as sure of this advice as any I've offered in seven books: Always define yourself in terms of lasting value to the client," writes Weiss. "When someone asks you, 'What do you speak about?' it's an amateurish question. But when you dignify it and satisfy it with 'I speak about x, y and z,' that's a career-limiting response."

Before I studied what Weiss had to say I would say things like I speak on marketing, I convey networking skills, I provide publicity advice, and so on. That's putting it in speaker's terms. Now I speak in buyer's terms. I say I improve lead generation, maximize revenues, reduce wasted marketing that erodes profitability, increase lead conversion rates and challenge attendees to exceed to higher goals. That's what speech buyers, the people who actually write the checks, want to have happen.

What is the value that you bring to the buyers of speeches? Not the participants, but the people who write the checks. This is the star that should guide you as you navigate your paid speaking journey. Speaking clients want their situation improved because of your speech.

"If you don't leave the client in a better position than the client was in before you got there," writes Weiss, "then there is no point in having you there at all."

CHAPTER 4: 30 TIPS TO FIND CLIENTS THROUGH PUBLIC SPEAKING

1. First, let's acknowledge a universal truth. Nobody likes public speaking. At least, not at first. Standing in front of a group of strangers can be nerve-wracking. Luckily, there's a cure, and it's simple: practice, practice, practice.

2. Few things make as much client seduction sense as speaking. Your prospects get to see you and hear you sharing expertise without any risk. Speeches are a perfect opportunity to be seen, heard, and most important, *remembered.*

3. Securing speaking engagements, however, is not as easy as throwing your name into a hat. You have to prove yourself and your credentials: A strong business track record, a unique message worth hearing, and compelling speaking skills.

4. If you need to learn how to speak, join Toastmasters. Not only is such a group likely to attract other success-oriented professionals, it's also a great, low-threat way to pick up practical pointers, watch other dynamic speakers in action, and begin to get used to the idea of speaking to groups.

5. Start with family, friends and colleagues. Just ask. As with other things in life, our circle of influence is often more connected to what we want than we might realize. Want to talk to local hiring managers at technology firms? Ask around and you might be surprised how many people in your network can suggest groups you might approach.

6. Package yourself. Write a one-page letter that explains who you are, what your background is, and three to five topics on which you are prepared to speak. Make this your standard "speech pitch." Also make sure you have a one-paragraph biography, introductory paragraphs for each speech, and a pre-written introduction (to YOU) available for the people who book you.

7. Prepare a 30-second commercial for your speaking. Condense what you have to offer to an audience as much as possible: "I'm Joann Blough, and I'm an expert on Tax Savings. I speak to more than twenty groups a year on unique tax

strategies, leveraging international tax law, and expanding tax savings through an international approach." Use this "elevator speech" when you network and socialize.

8. Buy a copy of a local directory of clubs and organizations. Most major cities have directories of active groups that use speakers. This kind of directory can be an invaluable resource when you're sending out letters offering your speaking services.

9. Contact group staff and committee members, who can tell you about each group's procedures for selecting speakers.

10. Contact university continuing education instructors in your field and offer to be a guest lecturer. Be sure to use handouts that are printed on your stationery that includes your phone number and Web address. Extended studies students are often more motivated, better educated and more attuned to forming alliances than the average person in the industry.

11. Or, get paid to speak—as a university extension instructor, or with such organizations as The Learning Annex.

12. Offer to do in-house training for corporations. It's a low-pressure way to hone your skills and really dig deeply into your subject of expertise. You'll also discover the need to make your speaking more interesting and animated when you're working with a group for a longer period of time—good lessons for anybody who wants to spend more time at the podium.

13. Approach conferences that are scheduled to take place in your area, or in your industry. Send them your speaker's introduction kit and topic list. Follow up with a phone call.

14. After a speech, offer to hold a small roundtable discussion for those who are interested. This can be later in the day, at a coffee break or over cocktails, and is a great way to solidify your position as a trustworthy expert, and to extend the impact and influence of what you've said to the larger group.

15. Consider going pro. The National Speakers Association (NSA) offers practice and networking for experts who get paid to speak. Once you're proficient at talking about your expertise, check them out and watch the opportunities expand.

16. When trying to woo and win clients, professionals and consultants need to remember that nobody loves a salesman. Just ask Scott Love. "The problem with actively selling your professional services to prospective clients is that it screams, 'I have no business right now,'" says Love, an author and an internationally recognized expert on leadership. "And if you have no business, how good can you be?"

17. Love maintains that prospects only want to do business with the sought-after and busy consultants, not the ones scrambling for new projects. How good can an empty restaurant be if no one is eating there? How good can a professional be if he has to actively solicit business?

18. "Instead of selling, focus on bringing the business to you by creating the perception that you are the premier expert in your field," says Love. "By following four practical steps your credibility factor will skyrocket."

19. The most effective way to build credibility is to create a perception that you are the "guru" in your field. Here are Love's four steps to accomplish that:

20. Step one: Target the industries in which you work. Clearly identify those industries in which your value is the highest.

21. Step two: Contact the associations that serve those industries. Initially speak to the editor of the association newsletter and offer articles that they can print for free on a subject in which you are an expert, something that solves a problem of their members or helps them raise the bar.

22. Step three: The association editors will never turn you down because they are always looking for good content. In fact, put several articles on your Web site as a collection for them to download at will. (For an example of how Love set this up, visit his Web site at www.scottlove.com.) Tell them that the articles are already written and they don't have to worry about deadlines because the work is done. Ask them to send you a copy of the publication and that they must print your non-salesy byline at the end of the article. "And don't make the byline a commercial," adds Love. "Have just your name, company name, what you do, and your Web site or e-mail or phone number."

23. Step four: Once your article is printed in their magazine or newsletter, contact the head of their education department or their meeting planner for their conventions. Tell them that you are an expert in your field and are recognized by many of their association members. In fact, tell them to turn to page 37 of this month's magazine so that they can see your article in it. Because you are in their very own publication, they will see you as an expert in their industry. Offer your services in terms of speaking and training for their association.

24. "Charge for this. Don't give it away," says Love. "If you don't charge for your speaking they will believe that you do not value your time or your message. Sure, they know you'll get business from it. But you need to charge for it." Love believes your initial refusal to give it away sends a message that you believe your message has tremendous value.

25. If it ends up that there is no way at all they will pay you, then negotiate something which costs them nothing, but has value to you. Ideas for free remuneration include: getting their mailing list, being a regular columnist in their newsletter, getting free advertising in their newsletter or a banner link on their site to yours,

obtaining free advertising in the conference program guide, receiving free sponsorship of an event, and having a free booth at their convention.

26. Whenever you can, charge money for your information. When people see that you value your time and your professional expertise, it sends a signal to the association, which is then conveyed to the rest of the industry.

27. "When you give your presentation, NEVER EVER sell your services from the platform," says Love. People hate that and will go out of their way for the rest of their lives to never do business with you if they perceive your breakout session to be a 90-minute commercial. Instead, give away all of your secrets and tell your audience that anytime they have a quick question that they can call you for no charge. (Be sure to put your phone number and Web site address at the bottom of every single page of your handouts). The ones that call you are the ones you want to talk to anyway, because they see you as the expert.

28. "And when they call, give them your best advice, letting them know in advance that you cannot spend more than just a few minutes off the clock with them," says Love. "They will then see the value of your expertise, and they will inevitably ask for more information on your services if they see a benefit."

29. "Follow these steps and watch your business explode," concludes Love. "By creating credibility in your firm, you will have a hard time keeping up with all the business that will soon seek you out."

30. Even though surveys consistently show that people would rather visit their in-laws than speak in front of a group, speeches and presentations are absolutely essential to long-term success for professionals and consultants who follow the Educating Expert Model.

Chapter 5: How Successful Marketers Attract All the Clients They Need

Management visionary Peter Drucker said, "there is only one valid definition of business purpose: to create a customer." To do this, a business must answer three classic questions: What is our business? Who is our client? What does our client consider valuable? (Drucker, 1954, *The Practice of Management*).

The number one challenge for small marketing services providers is creating new clients. Ironically, many marketing consultants feel marketing is too time consuming, expensive or undignified. Even if they try a marketing or business development program, most consultants are frustrated by a lack of results. They even worry if marketing would ever work for them. And no wonder. According to a researcher from the Harvard Business School, the typical sales and marketing hype that works for retailers and manufacturers is not only a waste of time and money for consultants, it actually makes them less attractive to prospective clients.

However, research has proven there is a better way. There is a proven process for marketing with integrity and getting an up to 400% to 2000% return on your marketing investment. At the New Client Marketing Institute we call it the Educating Expert Model, and the most successful professional service and consulting firms use it to get more clients than they can handle.

To attract new clients, the best approach is to demonstrate your expertise by giving away valuable information through writing and speaking. Research shows small marketing services providers can fill a pipeline with qualified prospects in as little as 30 days by offering advice to prospects on how to overcome their most pressing problems.

What should you do to increase revenues? First, understand that generating leads is an investment and should be measured like any other investment. Next, quit wasting money on ineffective means like brochures, advertising and sponsorships. The best marketing investment you can make is to get help creating informative Web sites, hosting persuasive seminars, booking speaking engagements, and getting published as a newsletter columnist and eventually book author.

Rather than creating a brochure, start by writing how-to articles. Those articles turn into speeches and seminars. Eventually, you gather the articles and publish a book through a strategy called print on demand self publishing (we've done it in under 90 days and for less than a $1,000 for clients). Does it work? Here are a list of business best-seller titles that started out self-published (Source: *Southwest Airlines Spirit*, March 2005):

- *The One Minute Manager* by Kenneth Blanchard and Spencer Johnson: picked up by William Morrow & Co.

- *In Search of Excellence*, by Tom Peters (of McKinsey & Co.): in its first year, sold more than 25,000 copies directly to consumers—then Warner sold 10 million more.

- *Leadership Secrets of Attila the Hun*, by Weiss Roberts: sold half a million copies before being picked up by Warner.

Even if you believe in the Educating Expert Model, how do you find time to do it and still get client and admin work done? No business ever believes they have too much time on their hands. Nothing worth happening in business ever just happens. The answer is to buy out the time for marketing. You need to be involved, but you should not do this all on your own. Trial and error is too expensive of a learning method. Wouldn't it be better if someone helped you who knows the tricks and shortcuts? We can show you how to leverage your time and get others to do most of the work for you, even if you are a solo practitioner.

How much should you invest in marketing? That depends on your business goals, but here are some norms. Law firms generally spend about 2 percent of their gross revenues on marketing, and the average expenditure is about $136,000. Marketing costs for accounting firms average about 7 percent to 10 percent of gross revenue (Source: *The New York Times*, November 15, 2001). The typical architecture, engineering, planning, and environmental consulting firm spent a record 5.3 percent of their net service revenue on marketing (Source: *ZweigWhite's 2003 Marketing Survey of A/E/P & Environmental Consulting Firms*).

Does the Educating Expert Model work? In the last 15 years we've had very good results guiding marketing services providers to increased revenues through more new clients, more fee income per client and more money from past clients. Here are just a few concrete examples:

- Through an informational Web site and electronic newsletter we helped create, one marketing consultant added an additional $100,000 in revenue from speaking engagements and sales of information products within 2 years

- In 45 days one client who is a marketing service provider for the home building industry was able to launch a Web site and education expert campaign that helped him double his business in a year

- Using one strategy alone a Web marketing business client was able to double his income and add $100,000 of revenue in one year through just one strategy

- By switching over to the model, a marketing services client was able to receive a 2000% return on investment from its new marketing campaign that featured how-to advice seminars and articles from senior executives

- When one firm gave up cold calling and switched to our model, the quality of their leads dramatically improved and closed deals quickly increased by 25%

- Using these strategies of seminars and getting published, a client has grown in a few years from a regional practice to a national firm

- A well established regional firm client reported they were able to accomplish more in 6 months with our methods than they had in three years on their own

- An advertising agency used the strategy to double revenues from $4.5 to $9.6 million in five years and earn a spot in the *Ad Age* 500

Please know this: the universe rewards activity. Start by asking clients about their pains. Gather information on how to solve those worries, frustrations and concerns. Be the expert who educates people on how they compare to their peers and the best ways to overcome their obstacles. The more prospects you inform how to solve their problems in general, the more will hire you for the specifics. In the words of motivational speaker Zig Ziglar: "You can get whatever you want in life if you just help enough people get what they want."

CHAPTER 6: SPEAK THE LANGUAGE OF INCREASE

You should read the best-selling works of the classic success authors such as Napoleon Hill, Clement Stone, Dale Carnegie, Og Mandino, Earl Nightingale, Norman Vincent Peale, Zig Ziglar, and today's leading success authors such as Stephen R.Covey, Anthony Robbins, Rhonda Byrne and Brian Tracy.

But if you want to go to the source, read a book that inspired all of these authors titled *The Science of Getting Rich* by Wallace Wattles. Byrne told a *Newsweek* interviewer that her inspiration for creating the 2006 hit film *The Secret* and the subsequent book by the same name, was her exposure to Wattles's *The Science of Getting Rich*. Byrne's daughter, Hayley, had given her mother a copy of the Wattles book to help her recover from a breakdown.

To attract clients, Wattles taught that we need to convey the impression of advancement with everything we do. In addition, communicate that we advance all who deal with us. "No matter how small the transaction, put into it the thought of increase, and make sure the customer is impressed with the thought," wrote Wattles.

Create the impression of increase if you want to attract others to you. According to Wattles, increase is what all men and women are seeking. His advice was that you should feel that you are getting rich, and that in doing so you are making others, like your clients, rich and conferring benefits on all who deal with you.

So when potential clients ask you what you do, please do give them a list of services and capabilities. Instead, use the language of increase to describe your marketing services. You can say that you:

- Improve lead generation

- Help clients maximize revenues

- Increase lead conversion rates

- Improve marketing productivity

- Reduce wasted marketing

- Enable clients to maximize prices

- Help marketing departments exceed goals

Add this language to your conversation, your Web sites and your proposals. This is what clients want. There are fortunes to be made by giving clients what they want. Back these statements up with testimonials that document the increase with numbers, percentages and time factors and you are way ahead of the competition. Here are some real (but not real names) examples:

"In one year all of the approximately 70 employees we have hired have gone through XYZ personality profile testing and candidate screening. This improved hiring process, combined with the improvements in our sales management leadership, has helped our company increase productivity per sales person a total of 21% in the last two years. In addition, while the national average for sales person turnover in our industry is 40%, we've been able to cut that in half with the help of this sales force testing and screening."

John Smith
President, ABC Company

"AAA agency has been working strategically with 123 Company partners for over a year now and they're an integral part of our partner program. We saw great success with partners in the program last year in terms of their retention rate of their new hires. The average retention rate of new employees brought on as part of that program was 70%, compared to the typical rate of 20%. Overall, the performance of the program more than doubled our first year expectations. We believe that this is due, in large part, to the work done by your firm, including the use of your profiling method and their active participation in the recruiting and hiring of the new sales people."

Maria Gomez
Director of Sales and Marketing
123 Company

"During the past 18 months our work with AAA Agency to train new sales people has helped us double year-over-year revenue growth and employee satisfaction. AAA Agency helps us understand if the candidate is right for us and then how to best to manage each employee to make them more productive."

Kent Clark
President, Big Company

Chapter 7: How To Fill Your Pipeline In Three Steps

Would you like to fill your pipeline with qualified prospects? Here is a three-step approach that works wonders:

1. **Identify Target Prospects**. Step one is to find a potential market niche that will be profitable. In today's market, clients demand specialists. You want fewer prospects to be interested in you, but much more intensely interested. This requires focus. It doesn't mean you'll turn down a client who doesn't fit into your two or three chosen verticals—it simply means you won't be actively shaping your marketing campaigns toward them. Evaluate your business. Have you sold most of your services to golf-ball manufacturers, pet stores, and electrical suppliers? Then THOSE are the three places to start thinking. But if pet stores in general don't have the budget for your services, you'll need to look harder.

2. **Make Prospects A Promise**. Step two is to determine what promise you or your firm is making to your target market. This includes your unique selling proposition: what you do, who you do it for and how you are unlike competitors—all in 25 words or less. What measurable results do you obtain for clients? You need to decide what makes you different than everybody else, and you need to overcome fear of focus—the desire to want to be everything to everybody. People hire consultants who specialize. Very few people would hire a surgeon who says he can do everything from tonsillectomies to facelifts and open-heart procedures. When you're in pain, you want a specialist—not just somebody who's "good with a knife."

3. **Harvest E-mails on Your Web Site**. Step three is to create an easy-to-update Web site that demonstrates your competence, rather than asserts how great you are. The Web site is the cornerstone of your marketing, and must not be a mere electronic brochure. Your Web site is the silent salesperson that prospective clients visit before making the decision to grant you permission to meet. There should be plenty of free articles with great how to advice for prospects. The home page of the Web site should have a headline that makes it clear who your target is and what pains you solve.

The Web site should include an offer a free special report in exchange for the visitor's e-mail address. This special report should contain valuable information that tells prospects how to solve their problem in general. Then e-mail these prospects tips and invitations to get more ideas from you at seminars, workshops and telephone seminars. Remember, the more people you tell how to solve their problems in general, the more will hire you for the specifics.

CHAPTER 8: CRACKING YOUR MARKETING GENETIC CODE

Is your marketing for clients pathetic or genetic? Pathetic marketing communicates the message that "I'm in business too."

Here is the *Reader's Digest* version on cracking your marketing genetic code. Before you can begin attracting clients, you need to create a marketing genetic code that is attractive to clients. All of your marketing messages, from networking discussions to speeches, will contain the elements of this marketing DNA that positions you as the Educating Expert. Here are 10 steps that will help you create these all-important marketing genes.

1. **Name your biz without your name.** Create a business name or a Web site name that gives potential clients a hint at the results you can produce for them. The worst possible business name or Web site name is your name. We know, we know, Ford, McKinsey and Price Waterhouse are named after the founders. But you are not them. At least, not yet. Sorry to say, clients don't want us, they want results.

2. **Boil it down.** Write a headline for your Web site and marketing materials that describes your audience and the results you produce for them. Do this in no more than 10 words.

3. **Name your client's pain.** What are your client's worries, frustrations and concerns that you help solve? This is also called the FUD factor: fear, uncertainty and doubt.

4. **How to fix it**. Describe your solution or methodology for solving these pains. What process do you follow to produce results? Offering a proprietary problem-solving process that you name and trademark is best. This answers the all-important question in their minds: "Why should I do business with you instead of one of your competitors?"

5. **The myths.** State the common misperception that holds many back from getting results. Why doesn't everybody do what you named in step 4?

6. **Step by step.** Tell your clients what they need to do in general to solve their problem. Pretend they weren't hiring you and you had to describe the steps they should take for success.

7. **The extras**. List any other benefits they get from following your methods. What other good things do people get when they do what you advise?

8. **Track record**. Elaborate on your track record of providing measurable results for clients. Be specific as much as possible. Use numbers, percentages and time factors.

9. **Give it away.** Create a Web site with free tips articles on how to solve these pains. Each article should be about 300 to 600 words. What's a good format? Consider the numbered tips approach you are reading right now (easy to write, easy to read).

10. **An offer they can't refuse**. Make prospects an offer of a free special report on your Web site. You are offering to trade them a valuable piece of information for their e-mail address. Tell them they will also receive a tips enewsletter from you. Assure them you will maintain their privacy and they can easily opt off your list any time they want.

Chapter 9: How To Make High Six Figures By Educating Prospects

What is It that you hate about marketing? You can fill your practice with desirable clients, without expensive brochures and humiliating cold calls.

If you are like many small marketing services providers, trying to find new clients can be frustrating. Maybe you are struggling with your marketing message. Or maybe referrals aren't paying off like they used to. Maybe you are concerned about wasting time and money on unproductive efforts. If marketing seems like a lot of hard work with little or sporadic payoffs, you are not alone.

How would you like to attract more clients than you can possibly handle, without breaking the bank? The good news is the American Dream of creating a marketing service provider business that provides a high six figure income is alive and doing well. That is, if you take the time to get the knowledge how to do it. Best of all, these techniques require a minimal investment.

Face facts. Other successful marketing consultants have found the way. How can you model their success? To attract new clients, the best approach is the Educating Expert Model that demonstrates your expertise by giving away valuable information through writing and speaking. In addition, you can increase closing rates up to 50% to 100% by discovering and rehearsing the right questions to ask prospective clients.

Here are the five ways prospects judge you (Aaker, 1995, Strategic Market Management) and my views of how the Educating Expert Model is the perfect fit:

1. **Competence**. Knowledge and skill of the professional or business and their ability to convey trust and confidence (you demonstrate and prove your expert knowledge by speaking and writing)

2. **Tangibles**. Appearance of physical facilities, communication materials, equipment and personnel (you do this by the appearance of your Web site and how-to handouts)

3. **Empathy**. Caring, individualized attention that a firm provides its clients (educating people to solve problems before they hire you proves you care)

4. **Responsiveness**. Willingness to help customers and provide prompt service (when you promise to give people things like special reports and white papers, do it promptly)

5. **Reliability**. Ability to perform the promised service dependably and accurately (prospective clients will judge you on how organized your seminars, speeches and Web site are)

CHAPTER 10: 27 STREAMS OF REVENUE FOR MARKETERS

To attract new clients, the best approach for consultants is the Educating Expert Model that demonstrates your expertise by selling valuable information through writing and speaking. In a matter of months you can have a system that positions you as an easily recognized and respected expert. This will most likely require two days of your time per week and very little of your cash.

- Do you realize how much you can make if you decided to get serious about growing your practice?

- Do you have a burning desire to grow your practice while making a high six-figure income and having fun doing it?

- Do you want to develop multiple streams of income that can create passive income and an incredible cash flow?

- Do you want more visibility and promotion to achieve that financial reward that so many other consultants have achieved?

If you answered yes to these questions, the answer is to develop multiple streams of income. Here are 27 streams to choose from:

1. Long-term retainers

2. Increased hourly fees (you probably are undervaluing your services)

3. Traditionally published books

4. Self published books (you can be a published author in 90 days)

5. Audio books

6. Profit-participation

7. Electronic books (you can be an e-book author in 30 days)

8. Industry specific training workshops

9. Tele-seminars

10. Webinars (online seminars)

11. Keynote speaking presentations

12. Membership Web site access

13. Being a rep for other products and services

14. Administrative services

15. Web-based distance education

16. Coaching/mentorship program

17. Adult continuing education

18. Compiled reference guides

19. Special reports and white papers

20. Paid syndicated column

21. Workshops at conventions

22. Form a trade association

23. Licensing

24. Direct mail newsletter

25. Multi-media products

26. Practice-building systems

27. Public open enrollment seminars

CHAPTER 11: HOW TO ENROLL MORE CLIENTS THAN YOU CAN HANDLE

How do you turn prospects into clients? Enrolling clients is different than selling products. Products are sold by professional sales people who typically don't see the buyer once the sale is made. But marketing services providers must enroll clients, which means building a personal relationship. Here, in a nutshell, is the four-step process for helping prospects enroll as your client.

1. **Make Those Calls**. Step one is to have set times in your weekly schedule to call prospects that have raised their hand. The objective is to make contact and determine if it is worth your time and their time to meet. Following a script outline can dramatically increase phone call success. But never talk about services or money at this stage (prescription before diagnosis is malpractice).

2. **Make A First Meeting Agreement**. Step two is to arrange meetings with potential prospects. A good diagnosis is the result of asking the right questions. You need to monopolize the listening, not the talking. Consultants must ask questions to uncover problems, budget and who makes the hiring decision. Not only is it polite to talk about money at this step, it is essential.

3. **Qualify The Prospective Client**. Step three is ask questions to make sure the prospect has pain, budget and a deadline to solve the problem. Then be clear on the next step before you leave the meeting and then confirm it with an e-mail within 24 hours. A common complaint of consultants is that this can turn into a game of hide and seek (the potential client now hides and you seek awaiting a decision).

4. **Make Presentation Meeting Agreement**. Step four is to never fall into the "send a proposal trap." You can waste considerable time and energy sending premature proposals. Trade a proposal for a meeting where you present. Sending proposals without meeting prospects is a game for losers (as in, you lose the business).

Chapter 12: How To Turn Pain-Into-Gain Teleseminars Into Increased Revenue

What do April, March and October have in common? These are the top three months for marketing service providers to host a teleseminar.

To make teleseminars fill your pipeline with qualified leads, first scrutinize your proposed topic by asking yourself some hard questions. If prospective clients attend this teleseminar, what beneficial information will they receive? Is this information that my competition either cannot, or does not, offer? Is this information a strong enough pull to justify them spending their precious time with us?

Next, examine how you spread the word. Do you have the right e-mail list for prospects (they gave you permission to e-mail them) and mailing list for suspects (these are strangers you don't know yet)? Maybe e-mail and direct mail alone are not enough to deliver enough prospects to your next teleseminar. A key to attracting high-level executives is to reinforce e-mail direct mail messages with phone calls. These calls also can provide valuable feedback on how prospects view the seminar topic and subject matter.

Event letters or invitations should be mailed or e-mailed approximately four weeks prior to the event. Another e-mail blast a few days before and event can also work well. Give registrants the option to call the 800 number, fax, e-mail or utilize the on-line event registration application on the Internet to register for an event. When possible, it is helpful to provide an overview of what will be covered.

Here are some business-to-business teleseminar scheduling guidelines:

- No business teleseminars on weekends

- Avoid Monday and Friday

- Avoid teleseminars in a holiday week (Fourth of July, June commencement)

- Check for conflicting industry events

The best months to hold a teleseminar in rank order are:

1. March

2. October

3. April

4. September

5. November

6. January

7. February

8. June

9. May

10. July

11. August

12. December

Telemarketing calls can increase registrations five percent beyond the registration rate from direct mail. Calling is conducted one to three weeks prior to the event. Many seminar experts recommend three calls attempts per contact with voice messages on the first and third attempts.

Typically, only 40-50 percent of those who say they will attend a free teleseminar actually attend. To minimize no-shows, confirmation e-mails are another option to consider. Send an e-mail confirmation 48 hours prior to the event. The e-mail confirmation will act as a reminder of the event and provide them date, time, location and directions. E-mail confirmations can greatly increase the attendance rate at the event.

CHAPTER 13: THREE HABITS THAT ARE KEEPING YOU POOR AND 10 HABITS THAT WILL MAKE YOU WEALTHY

It's a shame for you not to make great money as a business, when others do it so easily. Of course not everyone is doing it with ease. Most marketing services providers who have tried typical marketing are frustrated by a lack of results. After trial and error they feel marketing is too time consuming, expensive or undignified.

So they adopt the simple, dignified and easy approach. Here are three habits they adopt, but you should avoid:

- Relying on networking to find enough clients

- Hoping referrals will produce enough revenue

- Depending on a single stream of income

Fortunately many are learning the Educating Expert Model is the better way. Here are 10 Educating Expert habits to develop:

1. **Turn e-mail addresses into gold with an e-mail subscription link.** Offer prospective clients solid reasons for giving you permission to e-mail them; free reports, studies, white papers, or notifications of key Web site updates. And of course, state clearly that subscribers can easily opt out of your list whenever they want.

2. **Educate potential clients about how to solve their problems in general.** They will hire you as the proven expert to specifically apply your knowledge to their unique situation.

3. **Build a bridge of trust**. Give them valuable ideas on how to improve their business and their lives. Face-to-face seminars and speeches are best, then comes telephone seminars, online seminars and getting published.

4. **Hold free or low-cost small-scale seminars**. The best proactive tactic you can employ is to regularly invite prospects by mail and e-mail to small seminars or group consultations.

5. **Hold paid seminars and charge for your expertise**. Sell information products like teleseminars, workbooks, CDs and DVDs.

6. **Always collect e-mail addresses and send e-newsletters**. By signing up for your newsletter lists, prospects are telling you that they are interested in what you have to say but not ready for a relationship now.

7. **Your weekly reader**. Send e-mail prospects valuable how-to information and event invitations on a weekly basis until they decide to opt out of the list.

8. **Attend networking events and trade shows**. This is an excellent place to gather business cards and ask for permission to include them on your e-newsletter list.

9. **Get involved in community groups and associations**. Everyone likes to do business with people they know, like and trust.

10. **Get how-to articles published in client-oriented press**. Better than any brochure is the how-to article that appears in a publication that your target clients read.

Does this really work? Here are some measurable results testimonials:

"We saw 5 times ROI within the first 12 months we began working with you, and with your help we were able to double the size of our business in a little over a year."

Steve Fabry, President, Master Manuals, Inc.

"Your ideas in the past year on how to promote our services through educational forums like Webinars have been real winners. These events have boosted sales and helped position us as the thought leaders in our industry. The response rate for these online seminars has ranged from 2.1% to 7.5% and our return on investment to date has been more than 2000%."

Natacha Hosy, Harte-Hanks Market Intelligence

"My revenues for this year will be at least double to what they were last year. This program isn't for the faint of heart. You have to be disciplined and do what is recommended in a systematic way. And you have to add your own brand of magic to the equation. But the lessons you learn will deliver the results if my own experience is any indication."

Nancy Juetten, Nancy Juetten Marketing

"As a high performance coach for CEOs, I know high performance when I see it. Thanks to the help of Henry DeVries and the team at the New Client Marketing Institute I was able to add more than $100,000 in additional income in two years."

Boaz Rauchwerger, www.boazpower.com

"Your new-client-generating process has created a real advantage for us in the marketplace. With your coaching and program we've developed a very successful lead generation program that has produced more than 100 seminar attendees to date, along with a good increase in qualified prospects and conversion rates. Overall we estimate that our closed deals have increased by about 25%, and the quality of our leads has dramatically improved."

C. David Brown, Solutions Consulting Group

Chapter 14: The 10 Biggest Mistakes You Can Make Sending E-mail To Prospective Clients

Bad news. Your e-mails to prospects are not getting through. Open rates for marketing e-mails dropped 29 percent in a recent business quarter, according to a study by eROI. Click through rates fell 21 percent in the same period. Why did that happen?

This chapter is about the reason why, a four letter word that I am not going to use. The word starts with sp, ends with am, and we could call it special meat product that comes in a blue and yellow can. For this chapter, let's just call it smeat (not its real name).

What is smeat? Well, 96 percent of e-mail users define it as an e-mail "that intends to trick me into opening it;" 93% define it as "coming from an unknown sender." Many of us, myself included, are using smeat filters so we don't get so much of this kind of e-mail. (If you think I am being over the top calling it smeat, consider that even including the name of this "meat that shall not be mentioned" can trigger the filters).

So how do you maintain credibility with prospects and still prevent your honest e-mails and e-zines from being blocked? Here are 10 mistakes to avoid, advice culled from Web sites of the filters themselves.

1. Be open and honest and plain in your e-mails. If you try to hide things, or try to use tricks to bypass smeat filters, you'll look like a smeater and you'll be treated like a smeater. The statistics for use of these various techniques show that it occurs far more frequently in smeat mail than non-smeat, and the filter rules reflect that.

2. Do not use "cute" spellings, don't S.P.A.C.E out your words, don't put str@nge |etters 0r characters into your e-mails.

3. Don't include a disclaimer that your e-mail isn't smeat. Don't claim compliance with some legal criteria, especially one which is not actually law in your country. Only smeat needs to *claim* compliance — non-smeat is supposed to already be in compliance.

4. Don't type all in caps. A hallmark of the Nigerian Bank Scam, typing all in caps isn't just rude; it may get your e-zine forwarded to a blacklist. Additionally, make sure to capitalize the beginnings of your sentences and otherwise use professional grammar and punctuation. An unprofessional e-mail may be more likely to arouse the suspicions of your readers.

5. Steer clear of subject lines that scream SMEAT! Words like "free," "limited time," and "money" often trigger smeat filters (oops, hope that didn't trigger yours). Take a look at the smeat in your own inbox for examples of words not to use. Use normal conversational language, be sure not to use excessive spacing and or capitalization on your subject.

6. Make your policy clear. Tell readers how to unsubscribe at your Web site and in your e-zine. Let them know who to contact if they have any trouble. And, of course, make sure to follow through immediately. Offer directions for "subscribing" and "unsubscribing." Smeaters often use the word "remove" in their e-mails, so you'll want to avoid it at all costs.

7. Let's assume you won't include gratuitous references to smeat subjects. Don't talk about expensive watches, sexually oriented activities or drugs, or debt treatment, unless those topics directly relate to your e-mail.

8. Tell readers how you gather names (see the end of this e-zine for an example).

9. Send it from your own domain name. Free e-mail addresses are often used heavily by smeaters, so you'll want to stay away from them if at all possible. If your host doesn't offer mailing list capabilities, you may find ConstantContact. com to be effective.

10. Don't send attachments. Most e-mail readers regard attachments with suspicion anyway and the attachment may trigger smeat filters set up to screen adult material. Also, many of your readers will have limited inbox space; by avoiding attachments you won't give them an extra reason to delete your newsletter unread. (I am guilty of this but I am repenting. Soon when people order one of my special reports they will go to a hidden page on my Web site.)

CHAPTER 15: SOMETHING YOU PROBABLY DIDN'T KNOW ABOUT SEARCH ENGINES

For years we have been advocating that the best marketing you can do is to harvest e-mails from your Web site and then sending potential clients regular e-zines. In a way, this might be changing.

Want credibility with potential clients? Better finish high in search rankings. Forrester Research reported that 62 percent of search engine users click on a search result within the first page and 90 percent of users click on a result within the first three pages. Interestingly, 36 percent of search engine users believe that the consultants with Web sites listed at the top of the search results are the tops in their field.

According to Crain's B-to-B magazine, more than half of the marketers (52 percent) surveyed by MarketingSherpa described pay per click ads as outperforming all other tactics. This was the first time search ads surpassed e-mail marketing to a house list, which came in second at 47 percent.

Here are six simple rules suggested for effective search engine optimization.

1. **Love those free tools.** Become familiar with the free tools section of the Yahoo! Search Marketing Web site. This allows you to research how popular certain keywords are and if your competitors are bidding for these keywords.

2. **Make the first words count**. The first 150 words of your Web site are all important for the search engines. Make sure you use the two or three most critical keyword phrases in the critically important home page introduction.

3. **Consider your target keywords carefully**. Too many sites are relevant for a single word, so pick keyword phrases that are two or more words long.

4. **Don't use just the name of your business as the title tag of your Web site.** Failure to put target keyword phrases in the title tag of the Web site is the main reason perfectly relevant Web pages may be poorly ranked.

5. **Write interior pages with your keyword phrases in mind**. Add HTML hyperlinks to our home page that lead to major inside pages of your Web site. If you naturally point to other pages from within your site, you increase the odds that the search engines will find more of your Web site.

6. **Keywords are king.** Go to the three major search engines and search for your keyword phrases. Check out what Web sites are appearing in the top results. Visit these Web sites and then contact the site owners to see if they link to you. Links are often possible with non-competitive sites, especially if you offer to link back (often called reciprocal links).

CHAPTER 16: HOW TO WHIP YOUR LAZY WEB SITE INTO SHAPE

If your Web site doesn't fully engage visitors, you are not alone. But how to make it better without spending a fortune? The answer might be right in front of you at any shopping mall or grocery store.

Yes, you can use the science of stimulus response, also known as retail environmental psychology, to improve your Web site results. The trick is to tweak every page on your Web site to create a stimulus cue that affects visitor behavior. Just as environmental psychology has transformed retail stores like Nordstrom and Ikea (and many other commercial venues including casinos, malls, and now airports), you can immediately use many of these tactics to improve any Web site (not just those with e-commerce).

Face it, most Web site pages are lazy, but it is not their fault. That's according to stimulus-response expert Ron Huber, a principal with Achieve Internet of Southern California. The majority of Web sites never live up to their potential because the interior pages fail to motivate visitors to linger on the Web site and take action. Each page should have a role in persuading a visitor to do something and it should be clearly communicated on the page of what to do next.

In his landmark paper on Atmospherics, marketing sage Philip Kotler introduced the view that retail environments create atmospheres that affect shopping behavior (*Journal of Retailing* in 1973). Today most retail stores like Target, Whole Foods and Victoria's Secret rely heavily on environmental psychology research. Of course, the most-advanced proprietary research studies are trade secrets.

What are the lessons for your Web site? You don't necessarily need a new Web site, just tweak the one you have. According to environmental psychology, each Web page should offer the visitor a behavioral cue for what to do next. For instance in shopping mall design, the technique called the Gruen transfer refers to the moment when consumers respond to cues in the environment (named for Austrian architect

Victor Gruen). Like a Gruen transfer, each page should offer clear visual stimuli and navigation cues on what you action the visitor to take.

Here are nine common Web site stimulus-response mistakes that exasperate Web site users and hurt marketing results:

1. Frustrating navigation overloaded with unclear choices

2. Inconsistent look and feel past the home page or first level pages

3. Sudden unexpected changes, pop-ups or downloads when clicking on links and buttons

4. Web site doesn't collect names or encourage visitors to provide e-mails

5. Hard-to-find contact information

6. Baffling layouts that waste space

7. Little or no original content to encourage repeat visitors

8. Outdated information

9. No call to action directing the client to your optimal outcome

Want to discover a number of specific stimulus-response cues you can use to attract all the clients you need? Visit Ron Huber's Web site at www.achieveinternet. com.

Chapter 17: Five Ways To Increase Your Persuasion Power

To help prospective clients choose you, give them a persuasive mental shortcut. You can gain trust with clients through a proven persuasive secret called social proof.

With more than one quarter of a million copies sold worldwide, *Influence: The Psychology of Persuasion* by Robert B. Cialdini, PhD has established itself as the most important book on persuasion ever published. In this book that I highly recommend, Professor Cialdini explains why some people are remarkably persuasive.

The book explains six psychological secrets behind our powerful impulse to comply and how to skillfully use these tactics. The book is organized around these six principles of consistency, reciprocation, authority, liking, scarcity and social proof.

The principle of social proof states that one shortcut we use to determine what is correct is to find out what other people think is correct. As a rule, we will make fewer mistakes by acting in accord with social evidence than contrary to it. This is why television sitcoms have canned laughter tracks and commercials use man-in-the street testimonial interviews.

The reason social proof is so persuasive is because we are all so information overloaded. Professor Cialdini says his research evidence suggests that the ever-accelerating pace and informational crush of modern life will make automated decision making more and more prevalent.

"You and I exist in an extraordinarily complicated stimulus environment, easily the most rapidly moving and complex that has ever existed on this planet," writes Professor Cialdini. "To deal with it, we need shortcuts. We can't be expected to recognize and analyze all the aspects in each person, event, and situation we encounter in even one day. We haven't the time energy or capacity for it."

How should pain into gain consultants use social proof? The answer is testimonials with measurable results, and here are five ways to do it:

1. **Interview past clients to obtain testimonial quotes you can use**. Sometimes it is best to get an outside expert like a public relations professional or freelance writer to help you with this. You want to drill down to get measurable results. These include raw numbers (increased sales by $100,000), percentages (improved retention rates to 70%, which is triple the industry average) or time (accomplished more in six months than in previous three years).

2. **May I please?** Get permission to use the person's whole name, title and company name. Just saying "Sally from Kalamazoo" or Bob from "Cucamonga" just doesn't build trust.

3. **If you don't ask, you don't get.** Ask for testimonial letters on client letterhead that you can reprint and use in proposal packages being given to clients. The more you have to choose from the better.

4. **Tell me a story.** Ask clients who are willing to be your advocate to record their testimonial stories. One way to do this easily is to hop on a free telephone bridge line and have a service like Audio Strategies record the call. This can than be used as an audio file on your Web site or turned into a low-cost audio CD that you can give potential clients.

5. **Be a name dropper**. Pepper your speeches, seminars and presentations with accounts of individuals who have benefited from your service. Always make the person seem likable, describe the problem in brief and give a measurable result you helped achieve. One of my clients said he helped grow businesses. This became so much stronger when he was able to say he helped grow business by as much as 500%.

CHAPTER 18: A CHALLENGE TO THOSE WHO WOULD NEVER DREAM OF WRITING A BOOK

Being a published author is the quickest path to becoming an expert that attracts new clients. So why doesn't every business have a book?

Thanks to new technologies, today it is not only possible to produce a professional-looking copy of your book for under $1,000, you can also market the book through reputable sales channels.

A decade ago, there weren't too many options for consultants and consultants to get into print as a book author. If a traditional publisher wasn't interested in your manuscript, your only other option was to spend tens of thousands of dollars with a subsidy press or custom printer. And then, without ready distribution, good luck trying to *sell* the books.

But that has all changed because alternative publishers are able to print both paperback and hardcover books as they're needed due to the bold new digital publishing technology known as "print-on-demand." Going digital allows books to be produced in small quantities — even one at a time — almost instantaneously. No longer does publishing require behemoth offset presses, hangar-size warehouses, and fleets of trucks.

These alternative publishers have made a conscious decision to offer their services to everyone, rather than give control to an elite clique of editors and agents, as is often true in traditional publishing. While incoming manuscripts are checked for formatting before a new title goes online, alternative publishers do not edit for style and content. These consultants do not make value judgments about the literary merit of books. The author decides what the public reads, and the public decides if it makes good reading or not. It is a purely market-driven approach, and allows almost anyone to make a new book available to millions of readers, at a small fraction of the cost of traditional publishing methods.

There are challenges, of course. Because print-on-demand books are not typically stocked on bookstore shelves, authors need to do a good job of marketing through publicity, direct mail and the Internet. But if you are a nonfiction author willing to be a self-promoter and whose book targets an identifiable market, then alternative publishing may be right for you.

Print-on-demand has enormous implications for writers, readers, publishers and retailers. Because titles are produced "on demand," there are never wasted copies ("remaindered" as they used to be dubbed in the old days). Paperbacks and hardcover books are priced competitively, with authors receiving royalties of 30 percent or more. Compare those with traditional publishing industry standards of five to 15 percent, and the appeal becomes a bit clearer still.

What about the writing? If you can write articles, then you can write a book. And if you can't, hire a freelance writer to help you do it.

CHAPTER 19: HOW TO TURN STRANGERS INTO CLIENTS IN FOUR EASY STEPS

To attract new clients, the best approach is to demonstrate your expertise by giving away valuable information through writing and speaking. The trick is to offer advice to prospects on how to overcome their most pressing problems. Research client pains and tell them how to overcome them.

The good news is we don't want you to cold call strangers. In fact, that is the worst thing you could do. Try this instead.

Here is the four-step formula for turning strangers into clients. Some authors have likened this to moving potential clients up a ladder or through a funnel. Others have used sports analogies, like advancing the bases in baseball or moving the football toward the goal line. However you picture it, the idea is you are assisting these strangers to become clients by helping them progress through four distinct stages or groups.

1. **Group 1 are suspects.** The first step is to target a group of suspects. These are strangers who don't know you but you suspect they might be interested in what you do. Gather information about this group of strangers and the problems they have that you solve. Write a special report or white paper (fancy government term that means term paper) that offers solid advice on how to solve these problems. While you will be distributing this for free, your goal is to create something with information so valuable people would pay for it.

2. **Group 2 are suspects who have become prospects.** That's because they asked for a special educational report or information kit you created. Perhaps they came to your Web site for this offer. Or maybe they met you at a networking event and you got their permission to be put on your e-mail list. Trade your special report or White Paper for their e-mail. Create an e-mail database of those who are interested in your information.

3. **Group 3 are people who attend your seminars.** Invite group 1 by direct mail and group 2 by e-mail to attend events that you put on. These might be small-scale seminars or group consultations. Does it work? Lawyers at the top 1,000 firms, for instance, ranked seminars as the most effective tool for gaining new clients (Source: FGI Research, 1999). Create a separate e-mail and telephone database of those who attended your event and weren't ready for a one-on-one assessment consultation with you.

4. **Group 4 are people who met with you one-on-one and weren't ready yet to become clients**. At seminars offer a no-cost consultation to all those who attend your event. When you consult with these people, some will become clients right away. However, others might not be ready to become clients just yet. Create your separate group 4 e-mail and telephone database of those you had consultations with but they did not decide to become a client at this time. Keep following up with group 4 on a periodic basis. Keep notes on them so you can show personal interest in who they are and how they are progressing. The old adage about "many people don't care what you know until they know how much you care" rings true. The biggest mistakes consultants and consultants make is giving up too soon.

CHAPTER 20: HOW TO GET INSIDE YOUR CLIENT'S HEAD

What if you could get inside a potential client's head and see things from their perspective? If you could match how you sell your services to how they want to buy, then you would naturally be able to sell much more.

An incredibly accurate online marketing research tool is the online survey. Online surveys allow businesses to conduct professional market research surveys, get immediate answers and analyze the data in real-time.

Typically the surveys are hosted on the vendor's platform. In many cases a business can implement a simple survey for free; however, you'll have less options, including how many questions you can ask survey participants and how many responses you're allowed to receive.

For many of the free online survey providers such as SurveyMonkey, www. surveymonkey.com or Zoomerang, www.zoomerang.com, you can ask up to 10 to 30 questions and receive up to a hundred responses per survey for free.

However, if you want more, you'll need to pay. Still, even if you want more, prices start at just under $20 a month. SurveyMonkey charges $19.95 a month, which includes up to 1,000 responses a month, then $0.05 per response after. Plus, you can create and conduct as many surveys as you want every month. Imagine that you have a customer e-mail list of 200 people, and you're trying to determine what these 200 people need to help them increase their business, live a better life, earn money or whatever. You simply go to SurveyMonkey, write some questions and e-mail the link to participate to your customers. As your customers respond with their needs, you receive their feedback in real-time.

Another inexpensive online market research tool is the survey poll. Upon entering a Web site you see a box with a question and the option to select a true or false response. The process is automated, and depending on the script, will return the up-to-date poll results to the participant upon submitting their vote.

Why is this helpful? Polls are simple, fast and fun. They're a great tool to use to collect fast customer and prospect information. For example, if you're trying to decide between two titles for your next book, white paper, e-report or product, conduct a poll. Your poll could read, "Check which title you most prefer, [1] 6 Steps to Reducing Tension or [2] Reducing Tension Saves Lives."

CHAPTER 21: WAYS TO FIND CLUSTERS OF POTENTIAL CLIENTS

Are you struggling to grow your marketing service firm? The secret is to parlay your expertise into great business leads through speeches and seminars. Use public speaking to position yourself as an expert, obtain valuable publicity, build your reputation and even promote a favorite cause or issue.

You probably already know that public speaking, albeit a struggle for many, is the best way to build credibility. But did you know that speeches and seminars are also the best way to keep your pipeline filled with qualified prospects?

For starters, don't waste your marketing dollars on advertising and brochures that merely assert your competence. The best proactive lead generation strategy is to regularly demonstrate your expertise by giving informative and entertaining talks in front of targeted groups of potential new clients. The trick is knowing who to contact to get booked as a speaker developing a topic that will draw the right audience.

Want proof? In 1991 a random survey of the top 1,000 U.S. law firms found that 89 percent held at least one client seminar per year. In 1999, 94 percent of law firms were regularly holding seminars. Lawyers at the top 1,000 firms ranked seminars as the most effective tool for cross-selling and gaining new clients (Source: FGI Research, 1999).

Here are the top 15 places for the professional or business who speaks to find or create a perfect audience:

1. Small-scale seminars and group consultations that you host with 4 to 8 in attendance

2. Public seminars that you or others promote and charge admission to attend

3. In-house workshops that pay you to present to one company only

4. Local and national association meetings where you are a break out session speaker, panelist or a roundtable moderator

5. Radio and television shows that interview you for how-to advice

6. CEO peer group meetings like Vistage (formerly TEC), Inner Circle and Renaissance

7. College courses and extended education programs, like the ones offered through university extension programs

8. Public workshop consultants like The Learning Annex that pay you a percentage of the gate

9. Chamber of commerce events, from monthly breakfasts to special workshops and seminars

10. Teleseminars and Webinars that you put on or that others invite you to speak at

11. Promoter 50/50 seminars and expos where you are invited to speak and sell an information product, then split the proceeds with the person staging the event

12. Pre-recorded audio and video products that you sell on your Web site

13. Service club speeches to groups like the Rotary Club and Lion's Club

14. Multi-level marketing organizations that pull together people who sell for them

15. Churches that offer public programs

Here are some of the key benefits of promoting through public speaking:

- Allows your message to be heard above the noise of all the other marketing services providers

- Systematizes your marketing with a proactive approach that is simple and affordable to implement

- Makes it easier for your clients and business advocates to refer potential clients to you

- Creates multiple streams of income because prospects actually pay for you to market to them

- Produces all-help, no-hype marketing you actually feel proud to communicate

- Leverages your time so you get more results in less time

CHAPTER 22: THE EDUCATING EXPERT MODEL

The best marketing investment you can make is to follow the Educating Expert Model and offer helpful information to prospective clients. For example, billions are wasted every year on trade show marketing hype. Take the former Electronic Entertainment Expo (E3) for instance, once the world's largest trade show for entertainment and educational software.

As I was drowning in the ocean of marketing hype at one expo, I found a refreshing island of marketing help. What caught my eye was an ad with a college cheerleader wearing a "Hack U" tank top. "At Hack U, you will learn how hackers think, how they work, how they take revenue away from your games, and how you can prevent it," said the ad. "Come by our booth to grab a bite to eat and join us for one of our sessions."

"Hacker University" (good old Hack U) is the brainchild of Macrovision Corporation (Nasdaq: MVSN), a California company that helps the software industry protect and license software. A Macrovision white paper entitled the "The ROI of Content Protection for Games" was available for those who attended.

HackU provided timely coverage of the growing threat of game hacking, combined with its real-world impact on revenues. The hacker community's previous focus on PC and online gaming has expanded to include the Xbox and Sony PlayStation 2, further impacting game developer and publisher revenues.

Instead of just handing out logo pens and other trinkets (hype marketing) to the sea of passersby, Macrovision was able to engage potential clients in conversations about how to overcome the problems they face (help marketing).

Some argue that prospects today are bombarded with seminars, speeches and articles that contain generalities and do not distinguish the author or presenter from any of his or her competitors. The answer is a neglected tool: conducting proprietary research on topics of interest to prospective clients.

Macrovision conducted a survey of 9,000 video gamers showing that 21% of console gamers and 40% of PC gamers play pirated games. Most important, 73% of them would have purchased the game within one month if a free version had not been readily available. Thank you for the help. In business, that's something we need all we can get.

CHAPTER 23: THE MORE YOU LEARN THE MORE YOU EARN

So you want to build a reputation to woo and win clients? Some of the quickest reputation-building routes are to host seminars, give speeches and write articles. But why should potential clients listen to you? Like the old pastor once said, you can't save souls in an empty church.

Clients today are bombarded with articles, speeches and seminars that contain generalities and do not distinguish the business. Demonstrate that you have something to offer that your competitors do not.

Conduct proprietary research on topics of interest to prospective clients. You don't have to be a marketing research expert to pull this off. Here is a 10-step action plan to put this learning-into-earning strategy to work for you:

1. **Just ask.** Conduct proprietary research you can use in seminars and publicity. Remember those lectures in science class about the scientific method? Well, it's time to dust off that knowledge. The scientific method is about observing, forming a theory (or hypothesis) and then experimenting to test the results.

2. **Three big problems.** From your experience and observations, pick the three biggest problems you solve for clients and turn each problem into a research topic.

3. **Who cares?** Ask yourself: "Will this research be relevant to potential clients and trade journal editors?" If no, rethink the topic. If yes, proceed.

4. **Review the lit.** Surf the Web to review the literature of books, articles and published studies that relate to your research topic. Collect data through opinion surveys, focus groups, and analysis of case studies. Probably the best thing you can do is interview about a dozen people who match the description of your target client. Tell them you are using the information to write an article (you are).

5. **Analyze the data.** Then draw conclusions and make recommendations. Write a summary report on the findings of your research (this can be as simple as a report or as elaborate as a book).

6. **Tell everyone.** Use the research information in your seminars, speeches, how-to articles, Web site content and publicity.

7. **Your own problem-solving process.** From the research and your experience, create your own defined problem-solving system that will help you attract clients. Outline what you already do to solve client problems. Then break this process down into a series of defined steps (usually from five to seven are enough).

8. **Give the process an intriguing name.** The name should be typically no more than four words. Begin with "The" and end with "System," "Process," or "Methodology" for your proprietary process name.

9. **Your government at work for you.** In the United States, search the U.S. Patent Office Web site (www.uspto.gov) to find out whether you can trademark the name (steer clear if it's already been used in your industry). Seek legal protection of the process as intellectual property through the U.S. Patent Office. You can hire an attorney to help you or do it yourself based on the instructions on the Patent Office Web site.

10. **Leave some mystery**. Include the process on your Web site, but only give enough detail to describe it in general, so you have room to adapt it for each selling situation. Also include the process in your speeches, seminars and proposals. Continually improve the process, and be sure to document the improvements.

CHAPTER 24: HOW TO DOUBLE YOUR REVENUE

So you want to double your income? That's easy. Get a second job just like the one you have now. Oh, you want to double your income without working longer? In other words, increased cash flow and more time to enjoy it.

If you are a marketing services business, then you need to focus on the revenue formula. We don't know who your ninth grade algebra teacher was and what your relationship was with him or her, but please stay with us. This is as easy as A times B plus C.

A stands for new clients. B is how much you charge per new client. And C is the amount of money you get from past clients. So Revenue = (A x B) + C

Actually, there are two components to new clients: # of qualified prospects you talk to multiplied by your conversion rate. For marketing services providers, there are suspects, tire kickers and qualified prospects. Here are my definitions. A suspect is one of the 6 billion people on the earth you suspect might be interested in what you do, but all you have is a name and contact information. A tire-kicker is someone who has taken a step toward you to say they are interested in what you have to say. They may have attended a seminar, came to a speech, visited a trade show booth, signed up for your e-mail newsletter, asked for a copy of your white paper, or some other information gathering activity.

Now, a qualified prospect, that is a tire-kicker or a referral who calls you and wants to meet with you to hear how you might solve their problem (and how much do you charge). To recap, here are the formula components.

A = (#QP x CR%) = new clients
B = $ you get per new client
C = $ you get from current and past clients

To illustrate, let's say you talk to 10 qualified prospects per month. You convert 20% (1 out of 5) into new clients. You charge each new client $1,000. Added to that, you get $3,000 a month from existing and past clients. (Oh no, a word problem. Please, stick with me.) You make $5,000 per month.

$$(10 \times .20) \ (\$1000) + \$3000$$
$$(2) \ (\$1000) + \$3000$$
$$\$2000 + \$3000 = \$5,000$$

But what if you could talk to 15 qualified prospects per month instead of 10? What if you could get $1,150 per client instead of $1,000? What if you could convert 2 out of 5 (40%) instead of 1 out of 5? What if you could get $3,300 a month (10% increase) from past and existing clients instead of $3,000? All of these increases are actually modest and very doable. See what happens to revenue (yes, it more than doubles).

$$(15 \times .4) \ (\$1,150) + \$3,300$$
$$(6) \ (\$1,150) + \$3,300$$
$$\$6,900 + \$3,300 = \$10,200$$

How to leverage the four factors:

1. **Number of evaluators you talk to each month**. Hold seminars and teleseminars focused on client pain and research on how they compare to their peers

2. **Percentage of evaluators you convert into clients**. Use a lead conversion system where you ask the right questions (can increase conversion rates by 50% to 100%)

3. **How much you charge each new client**. Experiment with three-tiered platinum/gold/silver pricing strategies

4. **How much money you get from past and existing clients**. Ask about problems and offer options how to solve

CHAPTER 25: HOW TO DOUBLE REVENUES THROUGH ENDLESS REFERRALS

What is the best way to network with people at business functions, like Chamber of Commerce mixers or association luncheons?

According to Bob Burg, author of the bestselling book *Endless Referrals*, "All things being equal, people will do business with, and refer business to, people they know, like and trust."

One key to quickly establishing this type of connection is showing interest in other people by asking them questions. Burg has developed a series of questions to ask people at networking events that are not sales-oriented in any way. These are fun questions to ask and fun questions to answer.

While you will never need or have time to ask all of his questions during a conversation, Burg maintains it is good to have an arsenal to choose from. Here are four of his 10 questions:

1. *How did you get your start in the widget business?*

2. *What do you enjoy most about your profession?*

3. *What do you see as the coming trends in the widget business?*

4. *What one sentence would you like people to use in describing the way you do business?*

Burg's next question is the one that is key in getting the person to feel as if they know, like and trust you. "How can I know if someone I'm talking to would be a good prospect for you?" That final question shows you are concerned about them. You may be the only person who asked them this question during a first conversation.

Then, wrap up the conversation in another surprising fashion: Instead of offering them your business card, ask for one of theirs. Follow up by sending them a thank you in the mail containing your business card. These techniques might just land you in *their* database of preferred contacts.

In the newly revised version of Burg's bestselling book (over 150,000 copies sold), he updates many of the principles and techniques that resulted in ENDLESS REFERRALS becoming an underground hit within numerous niche sales industries such as network marketing, and insurance, and a staple for consultants new and veteran everywhere. For more information go to his Web site at www.burg.com.

CHAPTER 26: THE BIGGEST MISTAKE MARKETERS MAKE

What happens when you have a face-to-face assessment meeting with a potential client? You should keep track of your batting average: divide the number of qualified prospects you have an assessment meeting with (an at-bat) and by the number who become clients (hits). By learning to ask the right questions and listen, you can dramatically increase your batting average (new client sign up rates).

Questions should be your secret weapon. Questions persuade more powerfully than any form of verbal communications. Are you regularly practicing the right use of questions? If not, then you are making one of the three biggest mistakes that consultants and consultants make trying to attract clients.

Questions allow you to fully understand the prospect's pain. Pain is the difference between what prospects have and what they want, and as such can be classified as pain (things are bad and need fixing).

You need to ask open-ended questions to know the following:

- Does the prospect's motivation come from a problem that needs to be addressed today (pain), a problem that might arise in the future (fear), or simply an interest in getting more information?

- How does the problem impact the organization?

- How does the problem personally impact the prospect?

- How committed is the prospect to taking action to fix the problem?

CHAPTER 27: SPEAK UP AND FIND CLIENTS

Even though surveys consistently show that people would rather visit their in-laws than speak in front of a group, speeches and presentations are absolutely essential to long-term success for marketing services providers who follow the Educating Expert Model.

To turn speeches into clients, we recommend you read From Contact to Contract by Dianna Booher, CEO of Booher Consultants (a communication training firm that counts among its client list 25 of America's 50 largest corporations and 227 of the Fortune 500). Here are just three of her valuable tips.

1. **Make Subtle Mentions, Not Blatant Plugs.** A conference organizer's greatest fear is that a session will turn into a blatant sales pitch. "Your audience will protest loudly if your speech becomes a sales pitch," advises Booher. Still, you can (and should) create subtle ways to mention your services and organization. Choose case-based anecdotes to illustrate key points that showcase your expertise. Put descriptive slogans on your handouts and other reference material. And be sure to have the person who introduces you mention your organization and establish your credibility.

2. **Provide Multiple Avenues to Your Front Door.** When you do land a speaking engagement, you must give prospective clients in the audience as many ways as possible to contact you afterwards. In all likelihood, Booher points out, you won't be able to speak with each one or answer detailed questions immediately after the session. Instead, offer several methods to let them get in touch later. Put your contact information on slides, handouts, and invitations to future events. Give them a good reason to visit your Web site (offer a download of your slides or other free information). Make it easy and beneficial for the true prospects in your audience to seek you out.

3. **Be Stingy With Your Business Cards.** When a prospect asks you for your card after the presentation, turn the tables unexpectedly and ask for their card instead. Why? Because if you give them your card, you're dependent on them taking the next step. Booher points out that when you have their

card, you're in control of the follow-up process. Furthermore, she says, you should avoid exchanging cards, too, because that gives a prospect reason to say "I have your contact information; if I have a need, I'll be in touch." What you want, of course, is the opportunity to help them understand they have the need in the first place.

CHAPTER 28: LOW-COST AND NO-COST PUBLICITY TRICKS

Let's say you're watching the news. Ever wonder why certain consultants are constantly in the public eye?

In today's business world, media relations are not a luxury, but a necessity. That is the view of a great new book by Anthony Mora titled *Spin to Win*. He advocates consistently placing stories about your business in magazines and newspapers, as well as on the radio, TV and the Internet.

"We live in the communication age," says Mora. "If you hope to succeed, you need to communicate your message to the media."

You can begin by understanding the importance of promoting yourself. If you believe what you do is important, then it is of equal importance to let others know about it. If you don't, you are not serving your business, yourself, or the public.

"What good is it to offer a quality service, if no one is ever going to know it exists?" says Mora. "You may be an expert at what you do, but if it is not in some way brought to the attention of others, your career or business will assuredly fail."

Find Your Media Hook

Next comes your message. Coming up with a superb message for your professional service firm is simple, but not easy. What is it that you offer that makes you special? Why should your clients or patients come to you instead of your competitor down the block?

"Find your media hook. What makes you unique?" asks Mora. "Distill your message. Be clear and concise. The name of the game is communications."

Mora knows of what he speaks from experience. He began his media career as a freelance writer for such publications as *Us Weekly*, *Rolling Stone* and served as the editor-in-chief of *Impression* and *Excel* magazines. Since 1990 he has run his own Los Angeles-based media relations firm, Anthony Mora Communications Inc.

According to Mora, two or three people can run the exact same business — whether it is an accounting practice, a law firm, custom software company or group of management consultants — and the message behind each of these businesses can be completely different for each one.

"It is vitally important to understand your message, what you are trying to say, and what you are trying to communicate to your prospective clients," says Mora. "When approaching the media, less is truly more"

The book advises you to take a few minutes and write a description of your message and what you want to get across to prospective clients. Think of it as a brief mission statement that helps define you and your business. If you are a professional in a larger firm, this can be how you define your practice specialty area. Doing this brief exercise, says Mora, can help give you a clear vision of what you accomplish.

This isn't easy and the answers aren't always obvious. It may take time for some soul searching," adds Mora. "It is important that your audience, clients or patients realize that you are not just selling a service, but they understand the message behind it."

While the list is endless, here are some actual examples of distinctive messages:

- A construction company that offers doctors and dentists superior quality tenant improvements and better service than the competition.

- A management consulting firm that helps consultants accelerate business performance by improving the execution of strategic initiatives.

- A national law firm that exclusively represents management in labor and employment matters.

- A CPA firm that specializes in audits and reviewed financial statements for closely held consultants.

- A physician who offers patients traditional and alternative medical treatments.

- A sales training firm that rejects traditional methods in favor of a trust-building common sense selling approach.

Your list may be more specific that these examples, but it need not be. Once you begin to understand what your basic message is, you can begin to refine it.

"But that's just your starting point," says Mora. "Now you need to explain your message in a way that will interest the media and the public. How do you give better service? What do you offer that the competition doesn't? What unique services or benefits do you offer?"

What makes media placement effective, concludes Mora, is when it tells a story that educates the public on a particular topic that they otherwise wouldn't be able to access. Combine that with your message and you'll no longer simply watch the news, you'll be the news.

Is there such a thing as free publicity? The old adage says: "The sun comes up, and the sun goes down, and nothing else is free." There is a price to be paid for media coverage — you need to work on being newsworthy.

To be newsworthy, you must identify with the needs, wants, concerns and interests of your potential clients. Many consultants, entrepreneurs and IT consultants know that publicity is a cost-effective marketing method, but many miss the opportunity to garner "free" media attention because they don't know how to generate news coverage — or how easy it is to do.

However, if you are on a shoestring budget, there are the no-cost and low-cost ways of getting publicity.

1. Recycle, recycle, recycle your how-to advice

2. Fill your Web site with free how-to articles

3. Write reviews of all relevant books on amazon.com, barnesandnoble.com and list yourself as author/expert, owner of www.yoururl.com in your review

4. Put on seminars and list these for free in the newspaper calendar of events sections

5. Write an opinion piece that lists your book or Web site in the author blurb

6. Send timely, brief, and direct e-mail letters to the editor (e.g. editor@usatoday.com)

7. Start your own e-zine (electronic newsletter or magazine) and build list by trading free special report on your Web site for e-mail addresses

8. Gather business cards at events for your e-zine list

9. Join groups, take the membership list and send out an opt-out e-mail for your e-zine

10. Publish articles all over the Internet with links to your Web site

11. Sell how to articles to magazines (use the book *Writers Market* to find out what publications are buying)

12. Offer free how-to articles to magazines and newspapers

13. Send out news release on free Web news release distro service (Google to find them)

14. Get a gig as a columnist and then review others books (request help through www.profnet.com)

15. Attend events as a journalist (if you don't ask for a media credential, you don't get a media credential)

16. Give a speech by e-mailing friends to recommend you (how speeches get booked: 80% word of mouth, 56% hearing you speak, 46% speakers bureaus: source 1997 Walters Speakers Bureau)

17. Give a speech by calling and e-mailing strangers

18. Send a tips article to the newsletters of organizations you speak at

19. Teach a university extension class just for the catalog blurb

20. Teach a Learning Annex class just for the catalog blurb

21. Create information products and give away for free at speeches for cards

For Book Authors Only

22. Self-publish a book through Print On Demand (Author House, iUniverse, etc.)

23. Send out 300 review copies and you might get 30 reviews

24. Create a brag sheet about the book by soliciting blurbs and publicity and circulate to the media

25. Write a sample review of your book and send out as a suggestion to reviewers

26. Write a how-to article and send out with book to media

27. Write great cover letters to reviewers and include a hand written P.S.

Chapter 29: How To Win Clients and Influence Referrals

To attract new clients, the best approach is to prove your expertise by giving away valuable information through writing and speaking. Actually, that isn't technically true. You should sell the information if you want to win clients and influence referrals

Consultants can fill a pipeline with qualified prospects in as little as 30 days by offering advice to prospects on how to overcome their most pressing problems. But don't do it for free. Charge for your seminars and the information will be valued more by your potential clients. The burden is also on you to research great information.

This also helps those people who know, like and trust you enough to refer business to you. You can make these people a special deal: if they know someone who would value what you have to say, then your referral source can offer comp admission to your events on a space available basis.

Look what this does. You make the referral source feel special because they can hook people up. The prospects who attend still value the information more because there is a charge for it, and they feel even better because they didn't have to pay.

Unfortunately, many consultants who learn this truth find the idea of writing and speaking too daunting and even mysterious. Most feel this is only for a select few, but that is a miscalculated view.

First comes the problem, then comes research, and finally presentation. Dale Carnegie wrote that he had searched for years to discover a practical, working handbook on human relations. He started by reading every scholarly book and magazine articles he could find to ascertain how the great men and women of all ages had dealt with people. Then he interviewed scores of successful people and to discover the techniques they used in human relations.

From all that material, he prepared a short talk. He called it "How to Win Friends and Influence People" and it soon became a 90-minute lecture. Then the teacher learned from the students. Carnegie asked attendees to share their stories of how the principles helped them. First he put the rules down on a postcard, which grew into a leaflet, then a series of booklets, each one expanding in size and scope. After 15 years of experiment and research came the book by the same title as that original short talk. Of course, it has been a best-seller ever since (if you haven't read it, you really should).

During those 15 years of research Dale Carnegie became the go-to guy for human relations. Thousands attended his training each year and he prospered. This also resulted in many consulting contracts. He is long gone, but his training company has continued to this day.

So decide what niche you want to be the master of, then begin the research. As direct marketing expert and author Robert Bly once wrote, "Slice off a segment of the world's knowledge that you can realistically hope to master—and then convince others of this mastery." You can start small. You can start wherever you are. But by all means start now.

CHAPTER 30: HOW TO BUILD YOUR PROSPECT DATABASE

Are you in favor of free electrons? Once you have permission from a prospect to send them information by e-mail, you can woo them for virtually nothing. Here are 15 ways to expand your very important e-mail list and take advantage of those free electrons.

1. On your home page, make visitors an offer for your electronic newsletter or e-zine. Offer a bonus gift for signing up for the e zine, such as an ebook, special report, mini-course, or sample book chapter. The trick is to know your audience and create something they want.

2. In addition to your regular Web site, create a direct response one page mini-site. This should offer a different bonus gift to get people to join your e-mail list. Make a promise you will never rent or sell the list to anyone and they can opt out of the list any time they like. Typically mini-sites sell items such as information products (books, CDs, DVDs) or seminars and workshops.

3. Send targeted traffic to your mini-site through Pay-Per-Click search engines. Pay-Per-Click search engines are where you bid on the keywords terms related to your target market and are listed according to the highest bid for that keyword term. The two most popular are Google Ad Words and Yahoo Search Marketing.

4. When you give a speech, host a drawing. Ask everyone in attendance for a business card for the drawing and instruct them to cross their e-mail address out if they don't want to be on your e-mail list.

5. Find an affiliate to host and market a teleseminar with you. Offer to split the money you make from the teleseminar for access to their people. As part of the promotion invite the list to visit your Web site for the free bonus item.

6. Reach out to your target market by writing articles. By writing articles you show your target market that you know how to help solve their problems and may have a possible solution for them. This is the quickest way to build instant credibility in your niche. Post the articles on your Web site so the

search engines can find them and use free article submission services to place them on other Web sites and blogs.

7. Negotiate a sponsorship ad swap with an e-zine publishing peer. Contact other newsletter publishers. Let them know that you'd be interested to announce their newsletter if they're up to do the same for you. This way, both of you can build your lists faster.

8. Request that your subscribers pass it on. Word of mouth is a powerful viral technique that works great with e-mail marketing. If your subscribers find the content you share with them to be useful and informative, they will pass your newsletter on to their friends. This can be a good source of new subscribers.

9. Invite others to reprint your newsletter, as long as its content is unmodified. Many webmasters and newsletter publishers are actively looking for high quality content. If they reprint your newsletter, you will get new subscribers, traffic and links pointing to your site.

10. Include a "Sign Up" button in the newsletter. If you are using plain text instead of HTML, provide a text link to your subscription page. You may feel that this is not required, because the subscriber is already on your list, but remember that your readers will forward your newsletters to others, or reprint it online. You want to make it easy for them to subscribe.

11. Blog, blog and blog some more. Blogging is a great way to communicate with your potential customers, and it creates a nice synergy with your e-mail marketing. Be sure to include your newsletter sign up form on each page of your blog.

12. Use co-registration services to build your list. Co-registration is a great way to build your e-mail list. Your newsletter's ad appears on other Web site's and their visitors are able to check your subscription box and become added to your list.

13. Use direct mail to ask for e-mails. To improve on these efforts, you need to provide the recipients with a reason to release their e-mail addresses to you. Offer the bonus items they can get on your Web site.

14. When you telemarket, make sure that your callers have a script outlining the benefits to potential customers of providing their e-mail addresses.

15. Take your direct mail list and append e-mails. E-mail appending is the process of adding an individual's e-mail address to that individual's postal record inside your existing database. This is accomplished by matching the postal database against a third party, permission based database of postal and e-mail address information. Utilizing an e-mail appending service enables you to add e-mail addresses for up to 25% of your postal file, all within 3-4 weeks. (This is not a prospecting tool and should not be used with a list that does not know you.)

CHAPTER 31: BRANDING IS A BRIDGE BUILDER

Especially for marketers, your brand is your business. You need to shape every aspect of it consciously and carefully. When you build your brand well, you build a bridge of trust between yourself and your potential clients.

Every morning, people wake up with marketing problems. Other people (you) wake up knowing the people with marketing problems are out there, but not knowing how to find them. The Educating Expert Model is the art of building a strong, visible bridge between the people with pain—we'll call them Potential Clients—and the people with medicine to take away the pain (we'll call them YOUR FIRM.)

CHAPTER 32: MAKE A PROMISE

A first step is to determine what promise you will make to your target market. This is your unique selling proposition: what you do, who you do it for and how you are unlike competitors—all in 25 words or less.

If you haven't already, read *Positioning: The Battle for Your Mind and Marketing Warfare* by Al Ries and Jack Trout. For a good summation of positioning, we refer you to the classic text *Contemporary Advertising* by Courtland Bovee and William Arens.

Positioning will always be a buzzword in marketing and advertising circles. The authors demonstrate the concept by asking a few simple questions.

Who was the first person to fly solo across the Atlantic? Charles Lindbergh, of course. But who was the second? Not so easy?

Who was the first person to walk on the moon? Neil Armstrong made that one small step for man, one giant leap for mankind. But who was the second man to walk on the moon? The first person to occupy a position in the prospect's mind is going to be hard to dislodge.

For professional service marketing, it is critical that you earn enough recognition to make it onto the ladder for your category. The mind does not have the room for things new and different, so you must relate them to the old.

This is where nichemanship comes in. As an architect, you will be put on the architectural ladder. Frank Lloyd Wright is probably on the top rung. But you can be known as the architect who specializes in designing 21st century versions of Victorian homes.

Let's take law as an example. For years the top rung probably belonged to Melvin Belli, the attorney known as the "King of Torts." In her book *Expose Yourself*, former journalist turned public relations consultant Melba Beals describes how she helped create this positioning. But there is lots of room on the ladder. Describing yourself as the Melvin Belli of sexual harassment cases is not a bad strategy.

Start With a Guarantee

The Sears catalog built its reputation on it. Rolls Royce has become legendary by offering it. Federal Express transformed it from a begrudging obligation to a powerful marketing tool.

What is it? The extraordinary guarantee. And it just might be the key to substantially increasing your ability to woo and win clients.

One important book that should have changed the field of professional service firms and technology consultants (but hasn't, yet) is *Extraordinary Guarantees* by Christopher Hart, a former Harvard Business School professor and now president of a quality consulting firm. Hart's first effort to explain the value of guarantees was his 1988 *Harvard Business Review* article, "The Power of Unconditional Service Guarantees," which won the McKinsey Award for "Article of the Year."

Hart's book is a real eye opener. This is not just about Marriott Hotels and Domino's Pizza. In the book, Hart reveals why service consultants, which now account for 80 percent of the gross national product, have the greatest opportunity to differentiate themselves through offering a guarantee. He makes a strong case that extraordinary guarantees should be widespread for such professional service firms and technology consultants as law offices, management consultancies, advertising agencies, software developers, information technology consultants, and even investment bankers.

The vast majority of these firms, however, do not and will not guarantee client satisfaction. Why?

Risk...and Potential

Professional service firms, such as marketing services providers, generally perceive unwarranted risk in offering an extraordinary guarantee. Especially when they offer high-ticket services to a relatively small number of clients, even one client asking for its money back could be painful. And so, they refuse to guarantee their work. (As one humorist noted, sometimes the road less traveled is less traveled for a reason.)

"But there are reasons why guarantees can also be of exceptional benefit to these firms, especially in winning business of first-time buyers," says Hart. An extraordinary guarantee, well designed and implemented, actually reduces risk and creates value for clients, and this is key when fees can sometimes run into the six figures. When a firm knows that its fees are on the line, commitment to service quality increases—a development that benefits everybody.

"The greater the client's expected aggravation, expense, and time lost, the greater the power of the guarantee," says Hart. As he points out, while bad service at a restaurant can ruin your evening, bad service from a law firm can ruin your life.

Most firms are afraid to offer complete satisfaction. So, a strong guarantee can be the differentiator that makes you stand out in the client's mind.

But how do you make this work in practice? Find a way to fit the concept of a satisfaction guarantee into your own organization. What will you guarantee? Results? Process? On-time delivery? How will satisfaction be measured? At the end of the engagement? Monthly? Quarterly? Examining these questions thoroughly will do two things simultaneously: Allow you to re-engineer your own business to improve performance and ensure client satisfaction, and close more first-time clients by lowering their barriers and perception of risk.

1.   Five-Step Differentiation Worksheet

You should think in terms of your business plan when you're working out what's unique and different about your business. To that end, review the following questions and be able to answer them in depth. Our discussions on The Promise will grow from your initial thinking.

1.   Overview

- What is your company's strategic objective? How big would you like to be? What level of revenues? By when?

- Company strategic purpose (why do you exist?)

- Unique selling proposition (what is the difference?)

- Company story (what is your reason for being?)

2.   Growth Plan

- What are your growth goals?

- What are your assumptions? (i.e., rate of growth, period of time, capital required, operations adjustments needed, etc.)

- Timetable

3.   Management

- Management goals

- Organizational strategy

- Management team

- Personnel staffing plan

4. Marketing/Brand

- Marketing goals

- Overall description of market

- Brand positioning and image strategy

- Target market descriptions

5. Customer Satisfaction Plan

- Customer satisfaction goals

- Products/services descriptions

- Production strategy

- Service strategy

- Delivery strategy

- Customer service strategy

Once you've assembled all of the information above and can see "The big picture," work to boil it all down to what makes you DIFFERENT from everybody else out there who does what you do. One sentence is the ultimate goal, although you may not get there for a while.

Deliverable

The Promise. Start drafting your unique selling proposition. In this step, you concentrate on your business—you decide who you are, what you do, and what makes you different from everybody else only.

<Our firm> is a <specialized description> specializing in <services provided>. Unlike typical <generic company label>, we use a proprietary process and offer a 100% satisfaction guarantee.

CHAPTER 33: IDENTIFY YOUR TARGET MARKET

Before you can generate solid leads, you need to define, clearly and succinctly, your business. What kind of business are you? What do you do? For whom? What makes your services different from all the other providers out there?

You must also decide to target a market niche that will be profitable. In today's market, clients demand specialists. You want fewer prospects to be interested in you, but much more intensely interested.

Developing a plan to promote your business to a target market takes time, effort, and a dedication that most new entrepreneurs, or busy established businesses, think they don't have. It's important to identify the target audience, or the customers you intend to reach. Provide specific information about the people your company considers its clients. It's also important to identify user trends, or those changes in the market that can create opportunities for your company.

1. Do they have money?

2. Will they pay a premium for better service?

3. Are there a lot of them?

4. Is competition weak?

5. Can you easily get your message to them?

6. Do you already have credibility with them?

7. Do their issues interest you?

8. Do they know they need what you offer?

9. Are they geographically desirable?

10. Will they make good references?

You'll need some type of research to complete your plan, but have no fear—plenty is available. Secondary research is broad research that has been conducted by others, and is found at libraries and on Internet Web sites. Take advantage of it.

Now, add your target market to your developing "elevator speech." Remember, you're defining who you are, down to the smallest detail. You can't be all things to all people. They don't want you to be. People trust specialists, not generalists. They will hire you when they believe you have the knowledge and the experience to work with them, specifically.

Deliverable

Positioning. Continue to draft your unique selling proposition. Here, you insert your target market niches. This version will read much like the following.

<Our firm> is a <specialized description> specializing in <services provided> for , , and consultants. Unlike typical <generic company label>, we use a proprietary process and offer a 100% satisfaction guarantee.

CHAPTER 34: 6 STEPS TO NICHE AND GROW RICH

Is eavesdropping really a way to increase your chances for lead generation success?

As a child you were taught not to listen to other people's conversations. Or at least, not to get caught at it. For professional and technology service firms, discreetly eavesdropping can be a profitable activity.

Yes, it pays to listen to what clients want. An excellent book on the subject is *Niche and Grow Rich,* by Jennifer Basye Sander and Peter Sander. According to the authors, good niche service businesses are easy to start and easy to defend from competitors. By finding a niche where you can build your own stronghold, you can attract and maintain clients who will pay top dollar for your services.

Before you can generate solid leads, you need to define, clearly and succinctly, your business. What kind of business are you? What do you do? For whom? What makes your services different from all the other providers out there? Be a sponge to find these answers.

You must also decide to target a market niche that will be profitable. In today's market, clients demand specialists. To woo and win clients cost effectively, you will need to focus your efforts.

Developing a plan to promote your business to a target market takes time, effort, and a dedication that most new entrepreneurs, or busy established professional service firms, think they don't have. It's important to identify the target audience, or the customers you intend to reach. Provide specific information about the people your company considers its clients. It's also important to identify user trends, or those changes in the market that can create opportunities for your company.

Would you like a road map on how to size a niche market? Here is a brief synopsis of a six-step approach detailed in *Niche and Grow Rich* (the book includes useful analytic tools for each step).

Step 1. Define your market target. The authors say this means clearly defining the market niche, and its needs and key attributes. For example, "retired, widowed or divorced women, age 55 or older, unemployed, living in the wealthy suburbs of San Diego" might be a niche market target for a financial services firm specializing in estate planning.

Step 2. Define your service. Sander and Sander advocate relevance. They say it's particularly important — and useful — to define a business theme and position a service — with a value proposition — before going any further. A value proposition is what the clients will get from your service and what they would pay for it. You should be able to state this in a single sentence.

Step 3. Tune in to the market. Keep your ears open whenever you are near potential clients. What are they saying they want? The book shows you how to raise your antennae, tune in, listen and get a feel for the true needs and nature of the market. Tuning in to your potential market is a creative process that exercises all of your senses and mental faculties. Good listening often reveals slight twists or variations on the business idea or value proposition you probably didn't think about.

Step 4. Gather numbers. In marketing, a number is a valuable tool. Marketing and business plans are always more convincing if they have some real market data to quantify the size of a market. And with these numbers, you will feel better about the business idea.

Step 5. Determine growth drivers. What kinds of things would make a niche market grow? Part of the market assessment is to determine how much the business can grow, either naturally in the size of the niche or by "crossover" into other niches. If in the end you decide the niche is no-growth—but is captive and enduring—the authors say that's OK, but you should make that decision consciously.

Step 6. Start your financials. Recognize that market size and acceptance form the "top line" of the profit and loss, or "P&L" projection. When you have a grip on the size of your niche market and the sales potential for your service, the time has arrived to convert numbers into dollars.

Here is an example of a marketing service provider that knows their niche.

The Doctor Is In the Media

When it comes to wooing and winning patients for discretionary medical procedures, many doctors are finding it pays to be an expert quoted by the media.

Twenty years ago, the concept of medical marketing was unthinkable. Both the American Medical Association and the American Dental Association strictly forbade advertising and promotional activities. In 1975, after the Supreme Court ruled that antitrust law prohibited the American Bar Association from regulating how lawyers run their businesses, both the AMA and the ADA changed their stance, fearing lawsuits from physicians.

To gain trust with potential patients, many plastic surgeons have been implementing public relations in their practices for over half a decade. In fact, they were among the first medical specialists to use this method of practice promotion. Now, dermatologists, chiropractors, dentists, ophthalmologists, and others have followed suit.

"The editorial coverage that results from a successful public relations campaign can serve to make a plastic surgeon a star in his or her target area," says Katherine Rothman, CEO of the Manhattan-based KMR Communications, Inc. "Although good training, surgical results, and patient care is of paramount importance, in today's media driven society, women especially place tremendous credibility in what the media dictates as chic, fashionable, or of quality."

Rothman points out that public relations differs from advertising in that it uses editorial coverage in newspapers, magazines, radio, television, and health Internet sites to highlight a physician and his or her practice. Selected as "one of the top 50 healthcare PR firms in the nation" by *PR Week Magazine*, Rothman's firm has successfully represented dozens of plastic surgeons nationwide. Her clients regularly appear in prestigious magazines, newspapers, television and radio programs.

A public relations campaign can focus on new trends, techniques, controversies, safety issues in a respective sub-specialty or any host of topics deemed press worthy by a publicist and media representative. Essentially, a PR campaign works by taking information the consumer needs and wants to know and presenting it in the form of actual stories related to plastic surgery.

According to Rothman, the plastic surgeons who have created a name for themselves have not typically revolutionized cosmetic surgery, but more likely they have employed a publicist to create cleverly spun consumer oriented press releases which result in mentions in publications such as *Vogue, Glamour, Allure, In Style* and others of similar prestige.

"While medical advertising can sometimes translate as biased, it never occurs to the average person that a doctor employed a public relations firm to secure a media spot," says Rothman. "Not only can public relations and subsequent media exposure increase name recognition, it can also translate into actual patients and assure current patients that they made the right choice."

Ensuing media exposure in outlets such as *Elle* or *Vogue* magazine or programs like 'The Today Show' has a huge impact on prospective patients' medical choices. Rothman says it serves to reinforce that a physician is the expert in his or her sub-specialty. In addition, it lends a cachet and seal of approval that cannot always be achieved even by an aggressive ad campaign.

"But some health professionals still have a tendency to view marketing as hawking — much like a barker at a carnival or a crass used-car salesman trying to lure unsuspecting victims," says Anthony Mora, author of the book *Spin to Win* and president of his own Los Angeles public relations firm. "It's the thought of the coarse, smoke-and-mirror, hit-them-over-the-head style of publicity that understandably terrifies many in the medical field."

But just as the image of a physician giving a patient a stiff drink and a bullet to bite before performing surgery is archaic, says Mora, those public relations stereotypes have nothing to do with the reality of an intelligent, effective media campaign that educates and informs the media and the public. Used effectively, public relations can usher in new concepts and perspectives, and shape the ideas of a community and a nation.

"To reach that end, physicians need to view themselves as educators," adds Mora. "After all, we live in the information age and no profession, field or practice can avoid its effects. Professionals who understand the process and actively take control of the information are the ones who will succeed."

Today, savvy hospitals and physicians view public relations as an integral component of their business strategy. They are learning that they must change their perceptions to remain competitive.

Yet few have really come to terms with the process. Mora believes it's not enough to simply hire a professional and continue as before; a change in attitude and outlook is required.

For example, when it comes to communicating, doctors are used to presenting scientific data to their peers. They are trained to think in terms of studies and statistics, whereas the public and media both understand and respond more favorably to anecdotal stories.

Of course, this does not apply only to those in the health care field, adds Mora. Many professionals can speak the jargon of their particular field, but this makes for a very insular form of communication. He advises that all business professionals can benefit from learning to speak the public's language and honing their ability to communicate.

CHAPTER 35: CHECK YOUR REFLECTION

There are five attributes that clients use to judge professionals, and appealing tangibles heads the list. Tangibles include anything physical that will affect a potential client's perception of you and your company. This is where it pays to overspend. You never get a second chance to make a first impression.

Face It, We All Look Alike

As the old saying goes, experience is what you get when you wanted something else. So the trick is to learn from mistakes. Preferably other people's mistakes.

When it comes to wooing and winning clients for your professional service firm or consulting practice, don't make the mistake of looking like everyone else who does what you do.

"No matter what business you're in, you probably walk and talk a lot like the other people who do what you do," says Terri Langhans, author of a great new book titled *The 7 Marketing Mistakes Every Business Makes and How To Fix Them* and the founder of the marketing firm Blah, Blah, Blah.

Marketing consultants are a dime a dozen. An advertising agency is an advertising agency. Everyone knows a public relations consultant, and who isn't related to at least one graphic designer, if not by blood, then by marriage?

"Your target audience thinks your products and services, probably your marketing too, are pretty much the same as everyone else's in that category," says Langhans. "But here's the good news. The more two things are alike, the more important every tiny difference becomes in setting you apart, because the more two thinks look alike, the harder someone will actually look for a difference. They want to find something that will help them tell you apart."

Think points of difference. If everyone else zigs, maybe you should zag. Her message is to be a marketing maverick to get noticed. In fact "Maverick Marketing

Workshop & Round-Up" is the title of her "group therapy" seminar for business owners and marketing directors who want to stand out from the crowd.

Langhans obviously preaches what she practices. The former CEO of a national ad agency, she now uses her 20-plus years of experience to teach consultants through seminars and mentoring. She advises that you should resist the usual, the expected and the ordinary in everything you do.

While most speakers send meeting planners vertical flyers with large photos of themselves, Langhans gets noticed by sending a "card deck" of 10 business cards riveted together. Think "paint chip color wheel," except that each card has a thought provoking message from her maverick marketing mantra and a morsel of free advice on the back. Do the meeting planners remember her materials when she calls? Most of them have actually saved it.

"Naming my company Blah, Blah, Blah, instead of Langhans Something Or Other, hasn't hurt, either."

So how do you find your points of difference?

Start with all your points of contact, anywhere you come in contact with a customer or prospect, advises Langhans. These include:

- Fax cover sheet

- Voice mail greeting

- Front door

- Business card

- Parking lot entrance

- Reception area

- E-mail signature

- How you answer phones

- Proposal cover sheet

- Invoice

- Ads, brochures, flyers

"Look at what you're doing for each of your touch points, and then find out what the competition is doing for each of theirs," says Langhans. "If you have several competitors, you might need several lists. If you want to make it easier, just consider what most businesses in your category do for each touch point."

She says a good place to start is your voice mail greeting. Whenever Langhans speaks, she polls the audience to see if anyone does not know how to leave a voice mail. No hands ever go up. So why do we waste valuable time explaining to people how to leave a message when they hear a beep?

"Voicemail greetings all sound alike," says Langhans. "No one is listening to your greeting because they know what you are going to say. So take advantage of a free, easy, fast way to stand out in a big way."

Next, check your fax cover sheet. "If you're still using the template that came with your computer, your faxes look like eleventy-million others out there," says Langhans. "Tweaking your fax template could make a big difference, and while you're at it, toss out that Times default typeface, too."

Ah, but what to tweak them to? She says the single most important way you can set your business apart is the same way people are set apart. The difference is their personality.

Does your business have a conservative, upper crust personality? Do you see yourself more as a friendly, consultative family advisor? Or is yours an aggressive, yet precise and strategic persona?

All three can work. All three will attract a different type of client. But which one is truly you? Langhans cautions that you can't just pick a personality to try on. It has to be congruent with who you are and how you like to work. You can't fake a personality. Which is what makes it such a powerful marketing tool. Because your competition can't copy or fake your personality either. Once it's yours, you are one-of-a kind.

5 Reasons Why a Logo is an Important Part of Your Marketing

(Many thanks to Chris Cavanaugh, President of The Christopher Company, for this article on logos. You can find examples of The Christopher Company's work, more information about the company, and free resources at www.christophercompany. com.)

1. A logo differentiates your business from others visually, identifying the product or service you provide.

2. It creates a sweet spot, a point of familiarity between you and the marketplace.

3. It should exude authenticity. Customers crave what's real and genuine. A logo that looks like clip art demeans your business.

4. A good logo builds your brand. It's your promise to perform. And a promise is the heart of good advertising.

5. A logo is one of the most valuable assets of your business. The more it's used, the more equity it builds. And the more image and brand equity you

have, the more valuable your business becomes. This is especially important if you plan to someday sell your company.

7 Problems to Avoid When Designing Your Logo

1. Avoid using too thin of a line weight. Thin lines can disappear or break up in some publications.

2. Keep your logo simple and meaningful. If it's too abstract many people won't understand it.

3. Keep it balanced and in proportion. A logo designed in the wrong proportions for most applications will seem amateurish.

4. Stay away from fad typefaces that will soon be old-fashioned.

5. Steer clear of the obvious because it's probably overused. Resorting to visual clichés makes people think you're a cliché.

6. Putting a rectangular box around a series of letters is not very imaginative and could hardly be called a logo design.

7. Just because a logo is attractive doesn't mean it's effective. If it doesn't convey information about your business, it's not serving its purpose.

5 Characteristics of a Good Logo Design

1. An effective logo looks good small as well as large. It should have the same visual effect when printed on a business card or a billboard.

2. A good logo does not rely on color to be effective. Many times you can only use the logo in one color, such as in faxing or in the newspaper. That's one of the reasons why this guide is in black and white. It shows the logos in their purest form.

3. A good logo has a visual 'hook' that is appealing to the eye. Its unique design suggests that your business is also unique.

4. Ideally a logo should avoid using screens or graduated ink. In printing terms, a screen is a tint of one ink that makes it look lighter than the color at 100% value. In using a 50% screen, for example, the printed result appears half as dark. Screens are difficult to reproduce clearly and consistently.

5. An effective logo is simple rather than complex. Too many elements, or a logo that is too detailed or too complex reduces recognition and legibility, especially at smaller sizes. Express the idea about your company as simply, clearly and directly as possible.

Marketing Experts Comment about the Benefits of a Business Identity

"A logo is a visual representation of your company. This should look good at any size. A logo is a very important choice to make and should never be changed once you've decided upon a good one. Two million businesses are formed each year, and a logo will help you stand out from these."

Jay Conrad Levinson, *Guerrilla Marketing*, Houghton Mifflin, Boston, 1984

"Be careful to present yourself so that others' first impressions correspond to what you want . . . Wear your facade with pride."

Richard Koch, *The Natural Laws of Business*, Doubleday, New York, 2000

"Realize that your company is going to project an image regardless of whether you plan it or not. That image is either going to help or hurt you."

Richard White, *The Entrepreneur's Manual*, Chilton Book Co., Radnor, PA, 1977

Logo Design Process

How much time is spent on a logo depends on your needs. In all cases, there are a number of stages we go through to create your logo design.

Objective Meeting

What is your company's personality? Who are your customers? How do they think of your company? How would you like to be perceived? What is your principle product or service and what are its benefits? All this is drawn out during the objective meeting and taken into consideration. The amount of time spent in these meetings will vary. While one logo might require only a 15-minute phone call, another may require a site visit.

Determine the Type of Logo

Logo styles need to be considered and narrowed down to one or two types.

Concept Development

The phrase "Think Outside the Box" is used often but rarely understood. "The Box" is the limitation that designers place on themselves when they go with their first instinct or use someone else's less qualified opinion. Although the first idea could be the best, this cannot be known until other ideas are explored.

Thumbnail Sketches

Once an idea is formulated, the designer will generate a number of thumbnail sketches. The point of this Step is to get as many ideas on paper as possible without getting hung up on any particular one.

Roughs

The designer picks the best ideas and brings them to a point where they can be presented. This could be done on paper, at the computer or both.

Refinement

The roughs undergo revision so the quality is polished to perfection.

Illustration

Often a logo involves the use of an illustration, which, in many cases, is created from scratch.

Typography

Typography includes manipulation of characters such as leading and kerning, and sometimes even the creation of a typeface. Each has a subtle effect on the quality, aesthetics and readability of the type. Beyond the basics, the characters of the type might be manipulated to create your own unique version of a typeface. If the type is integrated to form a picture, the typography can become a creative illustration in itself.

Presentation

A person-to-person presentation can help us quickly narrow logo choices, as we work to identify which design elements work best. We try to distinguish the scientific from the subjective by focusing on each element of the logo separately.

Symbol Selection

Examining the symbols alone — without accompanying type — can help determine its effectiveness as part of the logo. Nike's and Apple's corporate symbols have enough recognition to be used without the company names. If the symbol alone creates enough interest or recognition, then we're on the right track.

Symbol Refinement & Style Application

Once a symbol is chosen, it's a good idea to explore different illustration styles to match the desired personality of the company. This step also serves as the client's last chance to identify any features they find problematic. It's easier to be critical at this stage than later on.

Type Selection

Once the symbol and the illustration style are chosen, a typeface should be selected to complement the style of the symbol.

Type Refinement & Arrangement

The arrangement of a logo's elements will determine the overall shape of the logo and is an integral part of the overall design. While one company might have more use for a horizontal shaped logo, another may be better served by a vertical shape.

Color Studies & Selection

Even though logos should be effective in black & white, it's helpful to explore which colors work best with your new logo. This step allows the client to see how well the logo works with a particular color or a variety of colors. This step is saved for last because it is very easy to change the color of a logo.

Logo Delivery

We deliver the logo in both printed and electronic form — in the most common format for professional use. Most computer applications can import EPS vector files. Both the electronic files and stats print are delivered in a folder with detailed explanations.

Homework

Review, revise and, if necessary refine or redesign the most important of your existing tangibles.

- Logo

- Business Cards

- Stationery

- Office furniture

- Walls and décor

- Wardrobe

- Look and feel of printed materials

- Snacks (we fill a huge platter to overflowing with candies, chips, granola bars, and other nonperishable goodies. The platter sits in the middle of our conference room at all times)

- What else?

Consider the impression a stranger might have if she walked in the door for the first time and saw your tangibles.

Tangibles are everything you can see, hear, smell, taste, and touch. It's not just your logo and color scheme, stationery, letterhead, and business cards; it's also your signs, office space, furniture arrangement, accessories, décor, employee dress, demeanor, answering machine message...even the candy bowl at the reception desk.

What's working? What's not? What could be improved? How quickly? Do your tangibles say "Trust Me"?

Deliverable

Start planning now to optimize your tangibles. You may not have the budget right now to reprint all of your collateral, but put it on your list. Meanwhile, could you change the greeting on your voicemail? Add a bunch of fresh flowers from a local farmer's market to your reception area? Drop into the warehouse center and stock up on healthy snacks and an attractive dish to put them in?

Create a comprehensive assessment of all your tangibles. Some people might want to keep track of their findings in a database or spreadsheet; others may find a simple checklist is enough to get the ball rolling. If you find it helpful, you can use the following format.

Tangibles Plan

Item: **LOGO & Visual Identity**

Status: ☐ Matches ideal image   ☐ Needs Improvement

Improvement Needed: _____

Target Completion Date:_____

Item: **Stationery, Cards, Envelopes**

Status: ☐ Matches ideal image   ☐ Needs Improvement

Improvement Needed: _____

Target Completion Date:_____

Item: **Office Space (Building, walls)**

Status: ☐ Matches ideal image   ☐ Needs Improvement

Improvement Needed: _____

Target Completion Date:_____

Item: **Office Decor (furniture, carpets, lighting, color, flowers, artwork...)**

Status: ☐ Matches ideal image   ☐ Needs Improvement

Improvement Needed: _____

Target Completion Date:_____

Item: **Image Folder (See Chapter 9)**

Status: ☐ Matches ideal image   ☐ Needs Improvement

Improvement Needed: _____

Target Completion Date:_____

Item: **Employee Physical Appearance**

Status: ☐ Matches ideal image   ☐ Needs Improvement

Improvement Needed: _____

Target Completion Date:_____

Item: **Vehicles (if applicable)**

Status: ☐ Matches ideal image   ☐ Needs Improvement

Improvement Needed: _____

Target Completion Date:_____

Item: **Printed materials (if applicable)**

Status: ☐ Matches ideal image   ☐ Needs Improvement

Improvement Needed: _____

Target Completion Date:_____

Item: **Products and Packaging (if applicable)**

Status: ☐ Matches ideal image   ☐ Needs Improvement

Improvement Needed: _____

Target Completion Date:_____

Item: **Other**

Status: ☐ Matches ideal image   ☐ Needs Improvement

Improvement Needed: _____

Target Completion Date:_____

CHAPTER 36: FORMALIZE YOUR PROPRIETARY PROCESS

You gain enormous leverage when you formalize something you've probably already got: a proprietary problem-solving process that you will now name and protect by obtaining a trademark.

Your process should have an enigmatic name that prompts questions; you want to be asked to explain it. A proprietary process is not only a marketing asset that will allow you to charge more, but also will make your work less accidental and improve the quality of your service.

How To Win Clients With A Proprietary Process

When potential clients tell you their problems, they expect you to tell them how you can solve them. This is the moment of truth: The time you explain how you solve problems like theirs. After you suggest a solution, you want them thinking, "At last... someone who understands my problem and really knows what they are doing."

There's an old marketing saying that goes like this: "If you don't have anything unique to advertise about your business, then you should advertise your business for sale." To woo and win clients, you need a distinct problem-solving methodology for your professional service firm or technology-based service company. This is your proprietary process, an approach unique to your firm.

If you go to the Google search engine and type in "proprietary process," you will discover 13,000 entries as of mid-October, 2002. Obviously, the proprietary process, as a marketing technique, is gaining currency in the marketplace.

Nashville-based business consultant David Baker says one of the most common mistakes a professional service firm can make is not having a defined, proprietary process. Writing in his newsletter Persuading (available through his Web site, www. recourses.com), Baker highlights several reasons why a proprietary process is important.

"Process is differentiating, highlighting the uniqueness of your firm with a process that you own," says Baker. Other advantages he cites are that a process demonstrates your experience, makes your work less accidental and will even allow you to charge more. "Clients are always willing to pay more for packages than individual hours within a fee structure."

A good proprietary process, however, is never a cut-and-dried industry standard lifted from a textbook. Instead, it codifies a firm's particular method of problem-solving, typically identifying and sequencing multiple steps that often take place in the same, defined order. Furthermore, the completed process should have an intriguing name — one that you can trademark.

What are some of these intriguing proprietary process names? Here are a few to ponder:

- The I-Innovation Process

- The SupporTrak RACE System

- The NetRaker Methodology

- The Systematic Determination Process

- The Persuasion Iteration Process

- The Innovation Continuum Methodology

Don't worry if you don't understand what any of these processes do just by hearing the names: That's actually the point. A name that is unique enough to actually qualify to be trademarked will also create the opportunity to explain the process to potential clients.

Don't go overboard, however, and create a name that is all marketing hype with no real service substance. Sometimes a line from a movie says it all. Remember when every burger joint had a secret sauce? In the film *Fast Times at Ridgemont High*, teenage workers from various fast food restaurants reveal what goes into the "secret sauce" for their hamburgers. One says "ketchup and mayonnaise," and the other says "thousand island dressing."

Make sure that there some real problem-solving ingredients have gone into the secret sauce of your firm — your proprietary process — and that the name actually reflects your unique approach.

Let-it-flow-chart

Most clients are attracted by specialization first, and then by a proprietary process. Here are some recommendations to create your own defined problem-solving system that will help you attract clients.

1. Outline what you already do to solve client problems

2. Break this process down into a series of defined steps

3. (usually from five to seven are enough)

4. Give the process an intriguing name, typically no more than four words. Begin with "The" and ending with "System," "Process," or "Methodology"

5. Search the U.S. Patent Office Web site (www.uspto.gov) to find out whether you can trademark the name (steer clear if it's already been used in your industry)

6. Seek legal protection of the process as intellectual property through the U.S. Patent Office

7. Include the process on your Web site, but only give enough detail to describe it in general, so you have room to adapt it for each selling situation

8. Continually improve the process, and be sure to document the improvements

Create an internal blueprint

In addition to the process documentation you show your clients, you should have a detailed internal document on how you use the proprietary process. The truism about service businesses is that people come and go, but the process is forever.

According to Professor Christopher Lovelock of the Yale Business School, you should create a blueprint of your business's process, a visual map of the sequence of activities required to complete the process for clients. To develop a blueprint, you need first to identify all of the key activities in the service design and production.

Service blueprints clarify the interactions between clients and members of the firm. "This can be beneficial, since operationally oriented businesses are sometimes so focused on managing backstage activities that they neglect to consider the customer's view of front-stage activities," writes Lovelock in his book *Services Marketing.* "Accounting firms, for instance, often have elaborately documented procedures and standards for how to conduct an audit properly, but may lack clear standards for when and how to host a client meeting or how to answer the telephone when clients call."

How To Trademark Your Proprietary Process

Does what you sell to clients cost more than $1,000? To woo and win clients, you need a distinct problem-solving methodology for your professional service firm, consulting practice or technology-based service company. This is your proprietary process, an approach unique to your firm.

A good proprietary process, however, is never a cut-and-dried industry standard lifted from a textbook. Instead, it codifies a firm's particular method of problem-solving, typically identifying and sequencing multiple steps that often take place in the same, defined order. Furthermore, the completed process should have an intriguing name — one that you can trademark.

Are you safeguarding your intellectual assets? Protecting physical property — such as buildings and cars — is an obvious choice for most business people because these things are visible and tangible. We can all see it, stand on it or ride in it. But what about trade secrets, trade names and copyrights? Intellectual property is another matter, because it is not easy to see and much harder to value.

Annually the United States issues 100,000 patents, 60,000 trademarks and more than 600,000 copyrights. The system is beautiful to behold when it goes right.

"As an attorney who has helped protect thousands of products and services in the past decade, I also have seen the unfortunate consequences when things go wrong," says attorney Larry Binderow, a specialist in trademarks, copyright protection and domestic/international licensing and franchising. "The stakes are high because counterfeit and fraudulent use of intellectual property costs U.S. business more than $60 billion per year."

When a mark is registered by the United States Patent and Trademark Office, Bindreow recommends that notice of the registration be given by placing the familiar "circle-R" ® symbol adjacent the mark as used on labels or packaging, and in advertising or similar publications.

According to Binderow, it pays to know the proper use of this symbol (or an alternative form of registration notice) with federally registered trademarks, service marks, collective marks and certification marks.

Reasons for Using a Registration Notice

Display of a registration notice is not mandatory. Use of the notice is recommended, however, for the following reasons:

*   The notice advises the public of your claim to exclusive use of the mark on goods or services specified in the registration.

*   The notice advises the public that the word or symbol is being used to designate the goods or services of the registration owner, and not merely as an ordinary adjective or product name. The notice also serves as a helpful warning to newspaper or magazine writers to avoid using the mark as a generic term.

*   Should an infringement occur, failure to use a registration notice will limit recovery of damages or profits to the period when the infringer was aware of the existence of the registration.

Acceptable Forms of Registration Notices

The federal trademark laws specify the following three styles of acceptable notices:

1. ®

2. Reg. U.S. Pat. & TM Off.

3. Registered in U.S. Patent and Trademark Office

"I recommend use of the ® symbol because it is short and easy to insert without upsetting the graphic balance of labels, brochures, and other displays of the registered mark," says Bindreow. "Positioning of the notice is not critical, but the ® symbol is normally used as a superscript immediately after the mark. There is no required minimum size for the ® symbol, and a small, unobtrusive size is perfectly acceptable as long as it is legible."

Points to Check before Using a Registration Notice

Binderow warns that it is improper to use any of the above-listed registration notices with a mark until a federal registration of the mark has been issued. Mere filing of an application for registration does not authorize use of the notice. Similarly, issuance of a state registration does not authorize use of the ® symbol or the other notice forms listed above. In the interim, a permissible and recommended procedure is to use a™ on trademarks not protected by a federal registration.

Homework

1. The Process. Think about the process you use to initiate and complete projects for your clients. Make notes on the steps you already go through. You may find it helpful to try to explain your methods to somebody who doesn't already know what you do. Have them take notes.

You need to break your process down into a particular number of steps, in a particular order. As a general rule, some numbers work better than others.

2. The Name. The name of your process should make what you do sound complicated and valuable. Some examples: "The Persuasion Iteration." "The Integrated Differentiation Method." "The Progressive Deconstruction Process."

Deliverables

1. A written description of your proprietary process.

2. A unique and enigmatic name for the entire process.

3. Evocative names for each step in the process.

4. <optional> A flowchart or diagram of your process to use in presentations.

Chapter 37: Goldilocks Pricing

You wouldn't eat at a restaurant that only offered one meal. You wouldn't enroll your children in a college that offers only one major. You wouldn't subscribe to a cable service that has only one channel. Your clients are no different.

Give them a range of choices. No doubt you offer more than one kind of service or level of service; package these creatively in ways that will let clients feel in control of their buying. We use the terms "Silver," "Gold," and "Platinum" as shorthand; you can name your packages whatever you like, so long as it makes sense and implies a scale of value.

"Silver" packages are the lowest level of service you'll offer — bare-bones, no frills, pragmatic, and no-nonsense.

"Gold" packages add more features, or frequency, or services; they're the ones most clients will choose, because most people believe moderation is a good thing.

Finally, there's your "Platinum" package. This is the package that will attract the kind of client who shops exclusively at Nordstrom and Neiman-Marcus. This package is for the client who likes to say, "I'm worth it." You may not sell a large number of them, but when you do, you'll be satisfied that you didn't leave money on the table.

Finally, it's important that, regardless of which package your new client chooses, it's still guaranteed. If you can't offer a 100% satisfaction guarantee on Silver Package work, consider whether it's worth offering at all. Your reputation is at stake with every client at every level; if you can't afford to do your best work at your lowest price point, then you may need to consider raising your prices.

An Example

Company X, below, offers custom publicity widgetry. They offer clients three levels of service.

Which would you choose?

Platinum	You get... • Tickertape parade • Bells • Whistles
Gold	• Bells • Whistles
Silver	• Whistles

Most people, faced with such a choice, tend to purchase the middle option. "Bells and whistles are fine, and we don't need a tickertape parade," goes the typical thinking.

So, load your Platinum package up to the hilt, and rest assured that most potential clients are like Goldilocks. They don't want too much, or too little. They want to buy "just right."

Homework

Think about creative ways to package your services to arrive at a tiered service system.

Deliverable

A one-page description of your services, broken into at least two packages (and preferably three). Feel free to rename the packages to fit your branding, and make sure that everything included in each level of service is spelled out clearly.

CHAPTER 38: (RE)BUILD YOUR WEB SITE

Next, you create an easy-to-update, database-driven Web site that demonstrates your competence, not asserts how great you are.

The Web site is the cornerstone of the new marketing, and must not be a mere electronic brochure.

Your Web site is the silent sales person that prospective clients visit before making the decision to grant you permission to meet.

There are a thousand and one current books available on Web design, and a lot of free information available on the Web itself. Don't go it alone. Study, research, and make sure that you're designing a site that builds trust — give away lots of good, free information. Don't waste your users' time. Make it easy for them to sign up for newsletters or other free goodies. And think of the site as an investment, not an expense.

21 Must-Have Web Site Elements

Your Web site should be the cornerstone of your client seduction efforts. The site is your silent salesperson — the one with whom prospective clients visit before granting you permission to meet with them.

A top priority for any firm that competes in the professional services or technology space is to create an easy-to-update Web site that demonstrates your competence. As the Internet matures, content is slowly becoming more important, but it's amazing how many sites for such firms simply assert how great the company is, rather than helping prospective clients.

If client seduction is defined as the art of wooing and winning clients by giving away valuable information, what are the classic Web site blunders?

According to our best practices research, the three most common errors are Web sites that are too busy; web sites that feature little more than lengthy company histories and other information important to the company itself; and worst of all, a site devoid of meaningful, useful how-to information. Without how-to information, a Web site is just a glorified electronic brochure.

From a best-practices standpoint, here are 21 must-have elements for a superior Web site that begins the client seduction dance:

1. **A clear positioning statement.** Tell prospective clients, in as few words as possible, what you do, whom you do it for, and what results you achieve. If you have a proprietary process or an extraordinary guarantee, this is the time and place to mention it.

2. **Free resources.** The key to earning your prospective clients' trust is to demonstrate that you know how to solve their problems in general. They will hire you to solve specific problems. With that key fact in mind, your Web site should be filled with how-to articles, white papers and special reports that give away valuable information.

3. **Declare your specialization.** The number one attribute prospective clients hunt for is specialization, so put yours right up front. No successful small firm is "all things to all people;" figure out who you serve, and how, and put that information on the front page. Be sure also to describe the outcomes you achieve, such as decreased costs or increased revenues.

4. **Mission and philosophy.** According to our focus groups, you should include a mission statement, but keep it short and meaningful. Clients say they don't really care that much about mission statements, but if you can use one to further differentiate yourself, it's a good idea to do so.

5. **Contact information.** Don't make your prospective clients work to find you. Put your phone number on every page. Make it easy for prospective clients to e-mail you with requests for more information or a meeting. And definitely consolidate all of your contact information on one page, including address, fax numbers, and so on.

6. **Map and driving directions.** If prospects ever visit your physical location, then you must include a map and driving directions to your office. This will not only save you time, but is also another reason to have prospective clients poking around your Web site.

7. **E-mail subscription link.** Forrester Research studies show that converting prospects into clients via e-mail is 20 times more cost-effective than using direct mail. Once you capture their e-mail, why waste first-class postage? Offer prospective clients solid reasons for giving you permission to e-mail them; free reports, studies, white papers, or notifications of key Web site updates. And of course, state clearly that subscribers can easily opt out of your list whenever they want.

8. **On-demand materials (PDF).** What happens if a prospective client wants to tell someone else about you? The problem with a beautiful Web site is that is usually doesn't look so beautiful when the pages are printed. The way around this is to offer professionally designed PDFs, readable with the free Acrobat Reader. But don't just offer a standard capabilities brochure; we recommend your menu include a how-to guide or tips brochure that includes capabilities information.

9. **Proprietary process.** After specialization, clients look for a specific problem-solving process. You should create this process, name it, trademark it and describe it with reverence on your Web site.

10. **Seminar information.** The best lead generation topic you can employ is the seminar, briefing, workshop and/or round table discussion. Focus on the biggest problems that you solve for clients. Your Web site should prominently list upcoming seminars (to promote attendance) and past seminars (to promote your reputation as an expert).

11. **Privacy policy.** In a confidential business? Then by all means have a clear privacy policy that states you will never share contact information with anyone else.

12. **Legal disclaimer and copyright notice.** For ideas on legal disclaimers, look in the front on any non-fiction business advice book published today. You will see language that says the publisher is not engaged in rendering legal, accounting or other professional service and the information is for educational purposes. And protect your intellectual property—your site content and free resources—by taking advantage of de facto copyright laws. Post a standard copyright notice.

13. **Focus-specific Information.** If you are a specialist in a certain industry, like health care or real estate, then there'd better be health care or real estate information throughout the Web site (you don't want to look like a poser or a wannabe).

14. **News releases.** The Internet is the number one research tool for journalists today, so include news releases, fact sheets, firm backgrounders and longer executive biographies in one area.

15. **Public speaking.** List upcoming and past speaking engagements with industry and civic groups. This promotes your reputation as an expert and will also help you garner invitations for future speaking engagements.

16. **Job postings.** Create positive, upbeat descriptions of the stars you attract to your firm (some clients will go here to get a sense of who you really are).

17. **Key employee bios.** Keep these short—say, 50-100 words. Longer bios belong in the news release section.

18. **Client base.** This can be tricky, but it's important. If it is appropriate in your field to list marquee clients, by all means do so. If this is inappropriate, then describe the types of clients you work for in general terms (e.g., "A Fortune-500 Manufacturer of Paper and Consumer Products").

19. **Case studies.** Our focus groups tell us most prospective clients aren't particularly interested in case studies because they believe specific cases don't apply to them and their own problems. A better approach is to take information out of a case study and turn it into a how-to article.

20. **Referral mechanism.** Your Web designer can easily include a feature that makes it easy for someone to refer your Web site to a friend or associate.

21. **Contact mechanism.** The purpose of the Web site is to let prospects check you out and then contact you. Have a device that makes it easy for them to do so.

Deliverable

Working with a professional Web designer (don't succumb to the temptation to let your teenage niece do your Web site for you!), you should create or redesign your site according to guidelines that will maximize trust and minimize user frustration.

Building a site that works takes more than just opening the box and installing FrontPage or Dreamweaver. You'll need a targeted site architecture plan, a user-friendly visual design, a front page with text that reflects your work positioning, and a quick and easy way for users to find your free resources.* You'll also need the capability to gather e-mail addresses and other contact information from interested prospects.

It takes at least 6 weeks to put together a good skeletal Web site. Allow time and energy for the process to take shape.

No, you might not have them yet, but you will soon.

Chapter 39: Share the Wealth

It's high time to write articles on how clients can solve their biggest problems. These are used on your Web site and in your lead generation efforts. You need to give away information on how to solve problems in general so clients will trust you enough to hire you to solve their specific problems.

Ghostwriters in Disguise

If writing for you is, as a late *New York Times* sportswriter put it, "easy . . . you just sit down at a typewriter and open a vein," then the tourniquet for you may be a ghostwriter or collaborator.

Getting published is an important variable in the marketing success quotient. Don't let the excuse that you're not a good writer prevent you from earning a byline. A professional can take your rough notes, conversations, and ideas and turn them into something that's polished and well-written.

What is essential and can never be farmed out, however, is your ability to present quality information and ideas. Your material should spark an "ah-ha" in your readers and ignite them to reach greater heights. If you can prompt someone else to succeed, then you will have too.

But great writers don't come cheap. You may be lucky to find a good, hungry writer who is trying to break into magazines or book publishing who is willing to work on the come. But, typically, you'll get to work that way only once with that author.

Any writer who earns his or her living writing soon discovers that while he or she is writing for nothing, you, the expert, are earning a living in your field. You have an income and a book. The writer has only a byline.

Recognizing that writing is a profession only if he or she can earn a living, a good writer will charge an hourly or project fee to ghostwrite or collaborate. Fees vary, but an average hourly rate ranges between $50 and $200. Magazine articles may be written for as little as a few hundred to as much as several thousand dollars. And book proposals' flat fees, just for writing, can reach as high as $5,000 to $8,000.

Brainstorm Your Article Topics

Here is a proven method for developing the advice that you need. Pretend a reporter is interviewing you for this story. What wisdom would you be sure to include? Write it all down. After you have brainstormed the list, cut it down to five to twelve best points. Write these up as your how-to advice, adding a few words of analysis.

Headlines for 'How-to' Articles

by Joan Stewart, The Publicity Hound
Want to write a how-to article but can't come up with a topic? Start by naming the three biggest problems your customers or clients face. You've just come up with three ideas for three different articles. Be sure the topics tie into a service you provide, a product you sell, or a cause or issue you want to promote.

Once you've chosen a topic, it's time to select a title. Here's a list of possibilities. Simply fill in the blank, depending on what you've decided to write about.

- *A Part-Timer's Tactics for a Full-Timer's _____*
- *A Quiz: Test Your _____ Smarts*
- *Cash in on _____ Trends*
- *Chasing the Right _____*
- *Cool Tools for Today's _____*
- *Common Errors That Kill _____*
- *Discover the 7 Essential Elements That Guarantee _____*
- *Finding the _____ That is Uniquely You*
- *Good News for _____*
- *How to Bounce Back from _____*
- *How to Get Other People to _____*
- *How to Handle _____*
- *How to Make _____ Work for You*
- *How to Make Your _____ Dreams Come True*
- *How to Turn _____ into _____*
- *Mastering the Art of _____*
- *No More _____*
- *Part-Time _____, Full-Time Success*

- Questions and Answers About _____
- Straight Talk from a _____
- The Great _____ Dilemma
- The Most Beginner-Friendly _____
- The Last Word on _____
- The Amazing Solution for _____
- The Best and Worst Ideas for _____
- The Complete Guide to _____
- The Worst Mistakes You Can Make When _____
- Top 10 _____ Do's and Don'ts
- What's HOT and NOT in _____
- When Not to _____
- Your Must-Know Guide to _____
- _____ with Pizzazz!
- _____ and Grow Rich
- _____ on the Cheap
- 5 Ways to Get More from Your _____
- 5 No-Fail Strategies for _____
- 6 Secrets to Successful _____
- 7 Ways to Keep Your _____ Dreams Alive
- 7 Ways to Avoid the Most Deadly _____ Mistakes
- 8 Ways to Avoid the Worst _____ Mistakes
- 9 Formulas for Fantastic _____
- 10 User-Friendly Facts for _____
- 10 Tips to Jump-Start Your _____
- 11 Questions You Must Ask When You're _____
- 12 Tactics to Open Up _____
- 13 Tips That Will Make a _____ Smile
- 10 Time-Tested Tips for Becoming a _____
- 25 Quick _____ Tips to Use Now
- 26 Holiday Gifts for _____

Homework

Brainstorm at least 6 topics to write about for each of your target audiences. In an ideal world, your topics would fulfill all of the following criteria:

- **The material is interesting and valuable to potential clients**

- **You know a lot about the subject**

- **The information isn't readily available from your competitors or other sources**

Next, get to work creating the resources, either with a ghostwriter or by yourself. If you need a bit of help getting started, read the following articles.

Deliverables

First drafts of at least 6 How-To articles (500-1000 words) to post on your Web site. These will also turn into seminar topics, so it pays to research them thoroughly.

CHAPTER 40: MORE ON PROPRIETARY RESEARCH

What research can you conduct, collect, interpret, or own? You need to conduct research that you own. It will come in handy again and again, in print, on the web, and as you talk to clients.

Begin by choosing the three biggest problems your target client's face that your service can solve. What clients want to know most is how they stack up to their competition. Your specific answers from research will command client and media attention.

And The Survey Said...

Another publicity secret is that the media loves numbers. An easy way to generate news that will get your name out there is to analyze and report statistics. Give the media provocative numbers, and they will give you coverage. This is what we term publicity-generating research. This is how it works. Find a topic that relates to your organization. Commission an opinion survey. Then release the results to the media in a news release that offers your analysis.

Here are some other examples of proprietary research in action, all taken from USA Today.

- If you like steamy sex conversations over dinner, you're probably single, according to a survey of 300 men and women conducted by Sfuzzi, a trattoria with locations in New York; Washington, D.C.; Dallas; and Houston.

- The lowly penny has a big following with the public, says a Gallup poll. Of 750 adults asked if the penny should be discontinued, the con-cents-us was clear: 62 percent want to save the single-cent coin. The poll was commissioned by Americans of Common Cents, a group organized by the zinc industry. Pennies are made mostly of zinc and use less than 3 percent copper.

- A friendly, helpful staff is what 76 percent of patrons want at a fast-food restaurant, according to a Wendy's/Gallup survey of 1,029 fast-food consumers.

- People would rather pay $50 a month for insurance that includes a nursing home benefit than have free coverage without the benefit, says an American Association of Retired Persons study of 1,490 adults.

- Cleveland and Nashville are among the ten cities that will be hot for hotel development in the near future, say hotel real estate consultants Laventhal & Horwath.

How To Turn Research Into Clients

So you want to build a reputation to woo and win clients? Some of the quickest reputation-building routes are to host seminars, give speeches and write articles. But why should potential clients listen to you?

"Clients today are bombarded with articles, speeches and seminars that contain generalities and do not distinguish the author or presenter from any of his or her competent competitors," says former Harvard Business School professor David Maister. In his highly regarded book *Managing The Professional Service Firm* (a must-read book for all professionals), he discusses how to demonstrate that you have something to offer that your competitors do not.

The answer, says Maister, is a neglected tool: conducting proprietary research on topics of interest to prospective clients. This can be technical or professional in nature, or it also can be general survey research.

Advantages of proprietary research

By conducting proprietary research, you obtain special information that prospective clients can't find elsewhere. The foundation of client seduction strategies is to give away useful information that demonstrates to clients you have the expertise to help them. Giving away general problem-solving information is good, but it is not good enough.

The information that a potential client most wants to know is, "how does my company compare to others?" There is a hidden fear in the back of the mind of every executive: are we missing out on something? Nobody wants to be behind the learning curve, especially in today's rapidly changing business environment.

Maister, who reportedly charges $15,000 per day to counsel professional service firms on how to improve their business, recommends surveying a cross-section of executives in a given industry. Ask them to prioritize trends they worry about most, list tactics that are of the most use to them, and name devices they use. Then you can report rankings of the most threatening issues and most popular tactics. For enhanced credibility, some firms get client industry associations to co-sponsor and help guide the research.

Let-it-flow-chart

Remember those lectures in science class about the scientific method? Well, it's time to dust off that knowledge. The scientific method is about observing, forming a theory (or hypothesis) and then experimenting to test the results. Here is a flow chart to help with your proprietary research studies.

1. From your experience and observations, pick the three biggest problems you solve for clients and turn each problem into a research topic

2. Ask yourself: "Will this research be relevant to potential clients and trade journal editors?"

3. Review the literature of books, articles and published studies that relate to your research topic

4. Collect data through opinion surveys, focus groups, depth interviews and analysis of case studies

5. Analyze the data to draw conclusions and make recommendations

6. Write a summary report on the findings of your research (this can be as simple as a report or as elaborate as a book)

7. Use the research information in your seminars, speeches, how-to articles, Web site content and publicity

An Example

A San Diego company that uses this strategy extensively is Harte-Hanks Market Intelligence, a 30-year-old La Jolla-based firm that provides customer relationship management (CRM) services. The company recently conducted a survey of 448 large U.S. corporations to discover how they were implementing CRM programs.

Based on the survey, Harte-Hanks was able to report that one-third of these large corporations have a CRM program in place or will have one in place within the next 12 months. Of those implementing a CRM system, approximately 26 percent are using or building a fully developed in-house solution, while the balance are using a variety of external partners and software packages.

How did Harte-Hanks use this information? The results were published in a white paper that was offered to other large corporations through exclusive executive briefings. The survey content was the basis for speeches at industry conferences and was also used in a series of no-cost, invitation-only, online seminars (also called Webinars) hosted by Harte-Hanks. Finally, the information was used for publicity, both as a general news release on some of the major findings, and as the basis of a how-to article on the top ten successful CRM implementation strategies.

While employing many other marketing strategies, Harte-Hanks Market Intelligence has made proprietary research a key part of its ongoing lead generation system. Overall, the practice has positioned the firm as a primary source of valuable information for clients.

Harte-Hanks Press Release Examples

DRAFT 081002
FOR IMMEDIATE RELEASE

News Release
Media Contact Only: Chet Dalzell
(212) 520-3232
chet_dalzell@harte-hanks.com
Business Contact: (800) 456-9748

**HARTE-HANKS STUDY EXAMINES
'HIGH-PERFORMANCE' B-TO-B E-MAIL CAMPAIGNS**

LA JOLLA, CA – August xx, 2002 – While average business-to-business e-mail response rates are in the 1 to 2 percent range as measured by use of a click-through device, some e-mail campaigns can garner as much as a 25-percent response rate, reports a new study from Harte-Hanks (NYSE:HHS).

What separates the extraordinary e-mail campaigns from the ordinary? That was the purpose of recent Harte-Hanks research, conducted by the company's market intelligence team, which examined 515 permission-based e-mail campaigns to uncover the strategic and creative practices of successful e-mail marketing in 2001 and 2002.

The study primarily focused on business-to-business campaigns in telecom and technology markets that were designed by Harte-Hanks' clients and executed by Harte-Hanks from August 2001 to May of 2002. Based on this time period, here are click-through response rate averages and ranges, broken out by purpose of campaign:

Purpose of E-mail Campaign	Average	High	Low
General Marketing	1.5%	25.0%	0.2%
Market Research	4.2%	21.0%	0.5%
Sales Promotion	1.8%	10.3%	0.1%
Offline Seminar Invitation	0.8%	7.3%	0.1%
Subscription Offer	1.8%	3.8%	0.1%
Online Seminar Invitation	1.0%	3.6%	0.0%

"While many an e-mail campaign does fail expectations, the potential numbers — as measured by the highs — are still too good to ignore," said Randy Wussler, vice president of product development, market intelligence, Harte-Hanks. "For the same budget, an e-mail campaign can touch twice as many prospects as a traditional direct mail campaign. However, not all e-mail campaigns are created equal."

Based on the 515 e-mail campaigns in the study, Harte-Hanks researchers have compiled a list of the nine "best practices" that separate higher response-generating campaigns from ordinary ones.

Top Nine High Performance E-mail Best Practices

1. Integrated media messages boost e-mail click-through rates by at least 5 percent. Like any other type of marketing program, the more an e-mail campaign is targeted, the better response it will realize. E-mail marketing should not be viewed in a vacuum. Based on the experience at Harte-Hanks, integrating a telemarketing and direct mail program will boost response rate, from 5 percent to 15 percent, as measured in click-throughs. While one message might suffice, Harte-Hanks has found that an ongoing dialogue using integrated media will lift response with clients and prospects.

2. Personalization is key to high response. Craft messages based on information known about individual recipients, and segments of recipients. While much attention is given to one-to-one marketing, e-mail content crafted for segments perform well, too. For example, content crafted differently for executives in sales, marketing, and senior management will lift response better than the same message sent to all three business titles.

3. Be straightforward in the subject line. The call to action should be the backbone of your subject line, and should include words that describe the offer or reason for action. Such words as "free," "discount," "complimentary," or "this weekend only" in the subject line lets the creative move response. While marketers often worry about fatigue in their lists, that is not only a matter of frequency but also a function of being misled at the recipient's first encounter with a marketing

message. Hiding or cloaking the true intention of a marketing message feeds fatigue and undermines confidence.

4. Clarity of message, offer, and response means is required. Anecdotally, e-mail is opened, scanned and closed at rates faster than direct mail. So it's imperative that every message contain a clear, compelling call to immediate action and provide a transparent response mechanism. The time customers and prospects spend searching for a "reply" button or URL is enough to lose them — thus layout is critical as well as traditional direct marketing discipline and principles.

5. The sender should be a person, not a company. People also are more likely to open e-mail from a person, rather than from a company or some generic server address. Designate a sender.

6. E-mail messages must have a clear opt-out process. Permission is permission, but the choice to take that permission away must be clear to the recipient. The quickest way to earn the wrath of busy prospects and customers is to send an unexpected e-mail with no way for them to opt out. Having a prospect name by way of permission is not an excuse to duck an opt-out option — in fact, it violates Direct Marketing Association and Association for Interactive Marketing ethics guidelines — even for business-to-business and customer e-mails. Never leave a recipient feeling helpless and out of control; the ill will such a campaign generates could be devastating. Make it easy for people to leave gracefully, preferably with a one-click procedure backed up by an 800 number. More and more recipients are noticing which campaigns follow accepted opt-out practices, and they appreciate having the option — even if they don't use it.

7. A response device should be more compelling than a simple link to a home page. In most cases, an e-mail campaign with only a home page link generates higher Web site "hits," but that traffic can get lost after the home page. When using links it is better to have a landing page tailored specifically for the offer in the e-mail message. Still, even a landing page cannot overcome an offer that in itself fails to be compelling.

8. Short and sweet works. Plain text-based e-mails can be very effective if they are targeted, have a compelling call to action and are brief enough to be read quickly. HTML e-mails, if utilized, need to include the same clarity and brevity in organization to elicit response.

9. Saturation points for frequency are low and getting lower. During the research period, it appeared that the optimal frequency for receiving e-mail messages is declining — across all categories. Appropriate use estimates vary widely, should continually be tested, but generally fall within a range of twice a week to twice a month. Err on the side of caution to foster continued good will.

Founded in 1969 and acquired by Harte-Hanks in 1999, the market intelligence team at Harte-Hanks manages the CI Technology Database, a primary source of information on technology purchasing plans and platforms of thousands of businesses in North America, Latin America and Europe. Harte-Hanks, Inc. (NYSE:HHS), San Antonio, TX, is a worldwide, direct and interactive services company that provides end-to-end customer relationship management (CRM) and related marketing service solutions for a host of consumer and business-to-business marketers. Harte-Hanks and its CRM integrated solutions use technology as the enabler to capture, to analyze and to disseminate customer and prospect data at all points of contact. Its customer-centric models allow the company to be the overall solutions provider for driving traffic to a Web site, call/contact center, or brick-and-mortar location. With premier specialized offerings — direct agency capabilities to print on demand, Web page design to e-care, desktop database capabilities to systems integration, personalized direct mail to e-mail, proprietary software products to application service provider (ASP) solutions — Harte Hanks provides practical implementation of technology and understands the needs of clients and their customers to deliver best-of-breed solutions. Visit the Harte-Hanks Web site at *http://www.harte-hanks.com* or call (800) 456-9748.

News Release
FOR IMMEDIATE RELEASE

HARTE-HANKS RESEARCH: CRM STATUS REPORT, 2002

-Harte-Hanks research examines CRM ROI, data access, customer view & systems development approaches across many types of consultants-

LA JOLLA, CA - June 17, 2002 - A new Harte-Hanks (NYSE:HHS) survey of 464 North American consultants and their implementation of customer relationship management (CRM) solutions reveals that consultants are expanding internal access to customer data and the content of those data is more focused on revenue history than in a similar survey the previous year.

A team of Harte-Hanks researchers conducted interviews in April and May 2002, using a sample of consultants drawn from the CI Technology Database of Harte-Hanks. The survey comes one year following a similar survey conducted among 300 consultants.

One surprising finding of the CRM survey is the absence of return on investment (ROI) measures at many implementations — 44 percent reported no such measures in 2002, compared to 32 percent in 2001. However, between 37 percent and 52 percent of respondents indicated use of at least one customer-based ROI-type metric in 2002 — metrics such as improved customer service ratings, improved client retention rates, and improved profitability tracking by customer. Reported use of such customer metrics grew by 17 percent between 2001 and 2002.

"The future of CRM investment is dependent on how successful consultants document and measure returns today," said Gary Skidmore, president, CRM, Harte-Hanks. "To justify the expense of CRM projects, even in phases, a variety of metrics will be important to ensure continuation of CRM programs, engage users, and determine overall success."

Corporate users of CRM systems and data are extensive, and expanding when compared to the 2001 survey. Marketing departments (both marketing communications, 76 percent, and product marketing, at 62 percent) recorded the largest gains over 2001, while inside sales was the most often cited department for such usage for the second consecutive year, this year at 86 percent.

Among other findings in the CRM Status Report 2002 study:

- **Enterprise-wide** — External sales forces continue to have more restricted access than inside sales (64 percent have access in 2002) — an indication that legacy sales force automation solutions may not be replaced everywhere a CRM solution is developed. Channel partners have access to customer data in just 16 percent of CRM solutions, but this figure jumps to one in five solutions among those respondents that are planning to implement a CRM solution within the next 12 months.

- **A more limited "full" customer view** —The array of content provided for in CRM solutions appears to be more focused on client revenue sales/history (68 percent in 2002). Just 19 percent include product purchase history, and 13 percent include tech support and/or customer service history.

- **One in five solutions are in-house** — Twenty percent of CRM programs are in-house-developed solutions, with no commercial CRM software packages, and very limited, if any, outsourced programming. Among others, 76 percent said they are relying on a commercial CRM package that is being implemented by either in-house or outsourced development resources.

- **The data silo challenge** — The most significant challenge related to implementing a CRM solution is the presence of data silos within corporations. The survey reveals that 42 percent said integrating different data sources into a single data system is the top challenge, followed by training users to use the solution effectively (37 percent), and participation of different departments within a company (30 percent).

- **A corporate initiative** — In nearly eight of 10 implementations, CRM is a corporate, rather than a divisional or local initiative. The department most often given the primary responsibility for setting ongoing CRM development and enhancements priorities is information technology (44 percent), with sales (16 percent), senior management (15 percent), marketing (11 percent) and other departments (14 percent) cited. Among departments charged with developing a CRM management budget, this frequently is an information technology-funded initiative (54 percent). However, among those planning a CRM solution within the next 12 months, senior management is the most oft-cited financer, in 45 percent of the planned solutions.

- **With a cross-functional management team** — A cross-functional team is the most prevalent method for managing CRM projects, at 42 percent. Thirty-five percent utilize an individual product team, while 23 percent use a designated team inside a specific document.

- **Web and wireless access still down the road** — The ability to access customer data via wireless and Web media appears to be limited. Fifty-two percent of solutions provide zero users with Web access to CRM data. Just 17 percent enable Web access to more than 75 percent of the corporate user base. Still, 44 percent of those planning a CRM solution within the next 12 months plan to provide 50 percent or more of their corporate users with Web access to customer data, most often an XML-based solution. Wireless access is even more limited, with just 5 percent of respondents giving more than 50 percent or more of their corporate users wireless access to CRM information.

Among respondents, 59 percent of the consultants included facilities with 100 or more employees. Eighty-nine percent reported a CRM solution now in place, 6 percent were planning a CRM solution within the next six months, and 5 percent were currently building a CRM solution. In addition, 34 percent surveyed were manufacturers, 29 percent were in the services industry, 15 percent were retailers or wholesalers, 10 percent were financial or insurance consultants, and 4 percent were in the transportation or utilities industries. The balance was spread among several other industries.

A full report of the CRM implementations, The CRM Status Report 2002, is available from Harte-Hanks Market Intelligence for $495. Full access to the CRM Database of the CI Technology Database for one year is also available separately. For purchase information, contact (800) 854-8409, ext. 7205.

Homework

Think about the kinds of research you might conduct. Start by looking at your business' records; do you have historical data that might be interesting to others? What secondary research could you mine and reassemble? What kinds of surveys might you use to come up with interesting, publishable data?

Deliverables

1. A list of studies you can either conduct, create, or manage

2. A target deadline for starting and completing each one

CHAPTER 41: CREATE YOUR PRINTABLE PIECES

Finally, it's time to think about those print pieces you used to pay big bucks for. You know—the ones that most marketing firms want you to buy by the metric ton.

This time, however, you're going to minimize what you spend on actual printing by using print-on-demand and PDF technology.

Forget thousands of printed brochures. They're a colossal waste of money. They go out of date quickly, they sing your praises and boast rather than building trust, and what's more, they get thrown away. Quickly.

The Folder

What you need instead is an image folder, one that will not go out of date for a minimum of five years.

The folder itself is the item your potential clients will see—and judge. Therefore, it should be visually appealing, with full color, heavy cardstock, sturdy design, die-cuts for your business cards and no-spill pockets. It should also be a standard size (to fit in a file drawer) and contain as few words as possible.

There are several techniques that will ensure the folder has a long and useful shelf life.

- No local phone number

- No address

- 800 number

- Web site address

- Use color

- Few words

- Pockets for inserts

The Contents

Next comes the contents: Adaptable documents that you can place in your folder, customizing for the occasion. You may choose up to three target markets, and need materials to adapt to each one. This allows you to project an image of a specialist with a specific process for each target client base.

Typical contents:

- Firm resume

- How-to information

- White papers

- Guidebooks

- Short bios

- Reprints of articles

- Seminar invitations

The PDF

Finally, it's time to create that brochure—but you aren't going to pay to have it printed. Instead, create an electronic version that can be read by anyone with an e-mail address and free Adobe Acrobat software.

You can post the brochure on your Web site, e-mail it to clients and even use your own laser printer to create print-on-demand versions for those Internet-averse potential clients.

Homework

Get your marketing print materials in order. Set deadlines and meet them.

Deliverables

1. Your Image Folder

2. Folder Contents for each target audience

3. A PDF brochure

CHAPTER 42: TOP 14 WAYS TO GENERATE LEADS

Often professional service firm principals tell me they are frustrated with the quality of their marketing materials, they are concerned with their firm's low profile or they feel pressure because their efforts are not generating enough new client leads. Are any of these issues for you?

Many do not know there is a body of knowledge about what does and does not work in marketing professional services. A review of the works of Maister, Robert Bly, Alan Weiss and other experts reveals a recurring theme of what does and does not work in professional service firm marketing.

Here are the top 14 tactics that work, but in descending order of effectiveness (I like to save the best for last). You might not need anything after #8.

14. **Cold calling by a business development person (never a principal)**

13. **Video brochures or CD-ROMS that give how-to information**

12. **Printed brochures that give how-to information**

11. **Sponsorship of cultural/sports events that appeal to targeted clients**

10. **Advertising in targeted client industry publications**

9. **Direct mail**

8. **Publicity**

7. **Seminars (ballroom scale)**

6. **Newsletters**

5. **Networking**

4. **Community and civic involvement**

3. **How-to articles in client-oriented press**

2. **Speeches at client industry meetings**

1. **Small-scale seminars**

Book Your Suspects

Before they can be leads, they've got to be suspects. The world of potential buyers is like a miner's sieve; you're panning for the gold nuggets. And to find them, you've got to go through a whole lot of sand.

The first step is to find the names, addresses and phone numbers of people who you suspect might become a client. This database will become the cornerstone of your marketing outreach efforts.

Research shows that 50 percent of the success of the lead generation efforts depends on this first step.

Once you've obtained all this information, it's time to organize and manage it; you have options. You might need to explore the capabilities of such software as MS Excel, MS Access, ACT and/or Goldmine.

50 Ways To Find New Clients

Where will you find your next million-dollar client? For those professionals and consultants trying to turn leads into gold, you need to be constantly prospecting. But where to mine for those new veins of business?

Authors Sam Parker and Jim Gould have leveraged 30 years of combined experience to answer that question. They have created a specific resource guide that can take years off the new client research and discovery time for professional service firms and IT services firms of all sizes. The authors, co-founders of a leading Web site for sales and marketing professionals called justsell.com, have published an excellent guide titled 50 Ways & Places to Find New Business (you can order the book at www.justsell.com).

Aimed at helping professionals and consultants find new business they may have previously overlooked, the book is a guide to the best practices known by the experts in increasing new client lead generation.

"Our central purpose in writing 50 Ways and Places was to bring together a comprehensive guide of information that was previously fragmented and sometimes unknown to those who are responsible for bringing in sales," says Gould. "The material can fast-forward a person's knowledge on finding new business by more than 10 years."

Here is a condensed view of just 10 of the 50 ways and places to dig for clients:

1. **Contracts recently won press releases** — According to the authors, consultants frequently announce when they win a large contract. Contracts typically mean growth for these consultants and contracts are often for extended periods of time. Two widely used press release sites are Businesswire (www.businesswire.com) and PR Newswire (www.prnewswire.com).

2. **Moving announcements** — If the company is moving, growth is anticipated. Perhaps the opportunity will be in six months, but the company's action of moving to a larger space is telling those needs exist or will exist. Moves can be announced in local newspapers, as part of articles in local news, in public filing documentation and through press releases.

3. **Employment classified ads** — Every weekend, consultants advertise employment positions. Want ads, when read properly, can be a huge source of opportunities to if you are seeking new clients. For instance, if the company is recruiting a senior IT security specialist, then it's logical that the company is prepared to make further investments in IT products and services. Employment ads can be found in many places including local and national newspapers, on job Web sites and in trade magazines and publications. The top job Web sites include www.monster.com and www.hotjobs.com.

4. **New executives hired** — New executives hired by consultants create tremendous sales opportunities within that functional area. A new executive hire is a threat to the current service provider and an opportunity for new providers. Typically, the new executive is excited about making changes and the company is prepared to support the new spending for those changes. Consultants often announce new executive hires with a press release, in local newspapers in the business sections and trade publications.

5. **Venture capital firms Web sites** — Venture capital (VC) firms make investments in growing consultants. The consultants that receive these investments usually invest the money relatively soon in a variety of areas. Visit the Web sites of VC consultants and see their list of portfolio consultants. To find VC firms on the Internet go to www.vfinance.com or www.nvca.org.

6. **Customer lists published on Web sites** — Among other recommendations, the authors advise you to visit the Web sites of all your clients and see who they list as their customers. You may choose to mention in your communication with these consultants that one of your clients is ABC company. Do not misrepresent this information as a referral.

7. **Hoover's Online** — Hoover's Online (www.hoovers.com) offers free access to its database of both public and private consultants. The basic profile is called a capsule and gives you a quick overview of what the company does, contact details and the names of key people. You can search consultants by name and industry for a quick way to obtain a listing of consultants to call.

8. **Trade show directories** — Ask your clients at which trade shows they are likely to be an exhibitor. Alternatively, spend some time researching on the Web trade shows that serve the industries you target. Once you've identified trade shows, visit the event sponsor Web site. The Web site should have a listing of past and planned exhibitors.

9. **Association Web sites and online membership directories** — There is an association for nearly every typed of business or industry that you can imagine. Identify those associations to which your prospects and customers may belong. One of the better places to find a listing of associations (sorted by state or industry) is the American Society of Association Executives (yes, the association for association managers). The searchable database is located at http://info.asanet.org/gateway/OnlineAssocSlist.html

10. **Sales lead database and directory consultants** — this is a quick way to obtain a list of prospects that you can either mail or call. These consultants compile large databases of consultants form a variety of sources. Some of the consultants that sell lists and information include Dun & Bradstreet, Harris Infosource, InfoUSA, TrueAdvantage and Harte-Hanks Market Intelligence.

Homework

Think about the kinds of people you want to reach — the people who are good potential clients. What is their industry, position, company size, geographic location?

Deliverable

Obtain a list of these people.

Load it into a robust contact management system.

Get ready to roll.

CHAPTER 43: BECOME A JOURNALIST

You need to get published by submitting query letters with article ideas to trade journals that your prospective clients read. The sad truth about trade journal articles is that editors reject 90 percent for being too promotional and not including hard numbers.

It may be time to hire that ghostwriter. For specifics about how to complete this step, read on.

Magazines and Newspapers

So where should your how-to article appear? The answer is probably waiting for you in your in-basket. You likely already subscribe to the leading trade journals for the industries of your target clientele.

If not, you can use a resource that professional public relations people turn to every day: Cision's Directories, which list publication and editor information for almost every media outlet there is. Your local library will have copies if you don't have the budget to purchase them (as of this writing, a complete set of Cision's directories, covering newspapers, Internet sites, television, radio, and magazines, ran a cool $1,200).

How do you use Cision's? Start by building a simple spreadsheet or database of contact information for publications you think your story might fit in, including the right editor, if one is listed. Then start sending queries, using whatever format the editor has listed as a preferred contact method.

The Bylined Article

Here's some good news. Want your article to appear in *The Wall Street Journal*? That's not very likely, because that publication is almost entirely written by staff journalists. But for most trade journals, only about half of the articles are written by staff journalists. The other half are written by practitioners in the field.

This is a deal where everyone wins. The publication wins because it gets quality articles it does not have to pay for. The readers win because they get expert advice from in-the-know professionals and consultants. And you win because you get some of the most potent publicity you could ever hope for to build awareness for your firm.

However, not all trade journals and industry publications accept bylined articles (a byline is the journalists term for having your name appear with the title of the article, as in by your name). Flip through the pages and see if you see articles written by practitioners. If you are in doubt, read the blurb that appears at the end of the article. This should contain the person's name, title, company and how to reach them (either a Web site or e-mail address). Find that and you have found opportunity.

But what if you don't subscribe to the publications? Then do what all good public relations people do. You need to obtain a copy of Bacon's Publicity Checker from Bacon's Publishing Co. of Chicago. This is the publication that lists, by subject and alphabetically, the thousands of trade journal magazines and newsletters. There is a wealth of information about each publication. In addition to listing how many people read the publication, Bacon's also indicates if the publication accepts bylined articles.

Study The Trade Journal

Editors will only accept articles that provide information and omit the promotional language. This is not an advertisement that you control. If you violate this basic principle, the editor will reject your story. The good news and the bad news is that editors probably reject 90 percent of the how-to article ideas that are submitted; bad news if you make it too promotional, good news (less competition for you) if you write it like a staff writer.

Be sure to visit the publication's Web site. Many will include a section on guidelines for writers. This will give you valuable information about how to submit ideas, article length, style, format and other advice. Other publications will send you a sample issue and writer's guidelines upon request.

How do you find out who is the right person at the trade journal to send your article idea? Pick up the phone and call. Research indicates that turnover among editors may be as high as 1 percent per week. If the directory you have is six months old, it may be 25 percent out of date.

Send A Query Letter

Before investing time and money in writing a how-to article, pitch the idea to the trade editor first. This can be done with a short, compelling letter or e-mail. Once you have his or her go-ahead, you can interview your customer.

Once you've honed your angle, you're ready to approach an editor. Don't pick up the phone and call. Just as if you were selling any other product, you need to write a convincing, professional proposal. But don't worry, it doesn't need to be lengthy; in fact, the shorter the better.

Editors want ideas submitted in the form of a one-page letter called a query. They don't want to see the entire manuscript. And you're wasting your time by writing the entire article before you know if you have a salable idea or the specific slant an editor may want.

Query letters do three primary things. They:

- Demonstrate that you have a fresh angle on an important topic.

- Show that you have the ability to write an article in a way that will interest the magazine's readers.

- Prove that you are the expert to write it.

It's important that your letter not just whisper your idea in a boring business letter style. It must trumpet it in a way that will be music to the ears of an editor whose in-basket is deluged with proposals from professional writers, public relations agencies and others who want to see their names in print. Your first paragraph — the lead to your letter — should capture the imagination of the editor by painting a scenario with a real-life anecdote, offering a startling statistic, posing an intriguing question, or turning a phrase in such a way that it makes the editor want to know more.

Submit Your Article

Congratulations, the editor says the publication will consider publishing your article. Now what? When you write your article, here is something to ponder. Most trade editors are always looking for interesting case histories. Most want solid numbers to back up the story, but are willing to accept percentages (e.g., sales increased 44 percent over the previous year, expenses were cut by 56 percent, two out of three customers are now experiencing gains).

Perhaps the most difficult part of obtaining trade journal publicity may be selling your best customers on the idea of agreeing to be interviewed. The time commitment on their part is probably three to five hours during the next four weeks. They will want to be assured they won't be giving away any trade secrets. Probably about 1 in 4 will agree to share the information, data and procedures that you need.

Before you submit your article, be sure to spell check and fact check the document. Having someone else read and edit your article also is a must. Finally, be sure the word count matches the guidelines of the publication. If everything checks out, send that article. Most publications want the article sent via e-mail, so they can download the information directly into their computers.

Four Other Ways To Get Your Name In Print

Not ready for the full-fledged how-to article? There are other ways to see your name and Web site address in print. These were suggested by Martin Hill, editor of the *San Diego Business Journal*.

- **Write a letter to the editor.** According to Hill, these are among the most well-read items in a newspaper or trade journal, but editors don't receive as many letters as they would like. "Write a letter commenting on a particular business issue, a news event or a story that appeared in the publication," advises Hill. Letters should be brief and include your name, address and daytime phone number (in case they need to check a fact).

- **Write an opinion column.** Hill recommends you choose a topic you feel strongly about and argue your case in less than 800 words. But be careful. Columns that promote a specific company or product will not be used. Sometimes it is a good idea to send the editor a brief e-mail with a thumbnail of what you intend to write.

- **Suggest a story about a business trend you've spotted recently.** Send a brief e-mail to the editor and they will consider it when they make story assignments. Give your credentials on why you would be a good resource to be interviewed for the article.

- **Suggest a story idea to one of the columnists in the publication.** Typically columnists won't promote a specific product or service. But they do need spokespeople to round out a story. Always ask if they would publish your Web site address, but if they can't you understand. If you don't ask, you don't get.

Homework

Start converting your free resources and proprietary research into query letters that you send to the most relevant press.

Deliverables

A list of target media

A list of articles you could write

At least one query letter per month, distributed to your target media list.

CHAPTER 44: JOIN COMMUNITY/CIVIC/TRADE GROUPS

Be a joiner, but be selective about where you decide to donate time as a member of a committee or board. You should be genuinely interested in the cause and the group should include potential clients and referral sources.

Use your status as a board or committee member to seek advice from key players inside and outside the organization. Here are some recommendations to accomplish all that and more:

- Strive to join groups in which you are one of the few representatives from your profession or corporate rank, rather than organizations comprised solely of professional colleagues.

- Let someone convince you to join the group. Use him or her as an ally to become a leader of the group, but avoid assignments that require maximum work with minimum reward.

- It is more important to attend the social hour than the meeting itself.

- Do your homework before joining a group. Begin by forming a linkage with the key staff person.

- Joining the membership committee is a smart way to gain the favorable attention of the group's power structure.

- Seek out high-visibility assignments, such as ad-hoc committees that report to the board of directors.

- When you discover that an organization doesn't exist in an area where you want to form alliances, take advantage of a golden opportunity and form such a group.

Homework

Start by listing the organizations you'd genuinely like to serve in an active capacity. What are your interests? What charitable or civic activities do you enjoy? Next, narrow your list down. Which of those groups are likely to attract the kinds of people who would be potential clients?

Commit to attending several meetings of one or two finalist organizations before you join for good. The dynamics of each group are different, and you should be able to gauge how beneficial your involvement might be within the first couple of months.

CHAPTER 45: KEEP NETWORKING

To advance your career or build clientele, it's essential to take part in professional groups. Work toward becoming a leader of one or more clubs; do that by joining the right committee. Do some homework before volunteering. Determine the chairpersons and members of various committees, then join those comprised of people with whom you want to form linkages. Committees give you a chance to show off your stuff (not just swap business cards), plus an opportunity to get to know all of the members.

CHAPTER 46: SEND E-ZINES

You need to send out e-zines that prospects can use. This can be done in traditional printed format or in the more cost-effective electronic e-mail version (actually, each one has a time and a place).

- *It's newsletter to me.* Newsletters are great, *if they are newsworthy.* Newsletters are poor marketing investments if they are not read. Just throwing in the company news releases from the past quarter is not a good idea. Instead, stimulate your editorial thinking and identify topics with high reader interest.

- *To get their attention, try grabbing them.* How good are the lead paragraphs of your articles? The most important paragraph in a newsletter article is the first one. If you want to increase newsletter readership, you need articles with attention-grabbing leads. Here are a dozen lead paragraphs that grab attention:

  - alliteration
  - anonymous person (not their real name)
  - epigram or famous quotation
  - historical anecdote
  - humor/pun
  - paint-the-picture description
  - philosophical statement
  - poem/song lyrics
  - pop culture allusion
  - question/do you
  - quote
  - round-up of illustrations

- *Here's a tip.* Include stories with tips, trends and tactics. Newsletter readers always welcome tips on product selection, installation, maintenance, repair and troubleshooting.

- *News you can use.* Another winner for newsletter readers is a how-to article. Similar to a tips story, a how-to article includes more detailed information and instructions. You can explain how to use the product, how to select the right model or how to maximize performance.

Sample E-zine

"New Clients Now" e-zine

Feature article = 630 words, about 3 minutes to read

To Blog or Not To Blog?

According to Technorati.com, a recognized authority on blogging, there are currently 59.8 million blogs on the Internet. Are you one of them?

And just what is this thing called a blog? A blog, or weblog, is a regularly updated journal published on the Internet. Think of it like a diary. Some blogs are intended for a small audience; others vie for readership with national newspapers. Blogs are influential, personal, or both, and they reflect as many topics and opinions as there are people writing them.

Blogs are powerful because they allow millions of people to easily publish and share their ideas, and millions more to read and respond. They engage the writer and reader in an open conversation, and are shifting the Internet paradigm as we know it.

To woo and win new clients, one of the best things you can do is share information that demonstrates you are an expert. You don't need to convince a publication to carry your column. A blog lets you do that in an easy fashion.

It surprises me how many professionals and consultants still don't have a Web site. For zero dollars and five minutes of time they could be up and running with a live Web site. There really is no excuse.

For others with a Web site, updating the site with new articles is too much of a hassle. However, this needn't be the case.

Bloggers frequently link to and comment on other blogs, creating the type of immediate connection one would have in a conversation. Technorati tracks these links, and thus the relative relevance of blogs, photos, videos etc. They rapidly index tens of thousands of updates every hour, and so we monitor these live communities and the conversations they foster.

The World Wide Web is incredibly active, and according to Technorati data, there are over 175,000 new blogs (that's just blogs) every day. Bloggers update their blogs regularly to the tune of over 1.6 million posts per day, or over 18 updates a second.

According to Wikipedia, an online encyclopedia that is mostly correct, early weblogs were simply manually updated components of common Web sites. You can still do this by just updating your free article or what's new section of your Web site.

However, the evolution of tools to facilitate the production and maintenance of web articles posted in said chronological fashion made the publishing process feasible to a much larger, less technical, population. Ultimately, this resulted in the distinct class of online publishing that produces blogs we recognize today. For instance, the use of some sort of browser-based software is now a typical aspect of "blogging." Blogs can be hosted by dedicated blog hosting services, or they can be run using blog software, such as WordPress, blogger or LiveJournal, or on regular Web hosting services, such as DreamHost.

If you don't have a blog yet, check out the blogger.com Web site. Blogger was started by a tiny company in San Francisco called Pyra Labs in August of 1999. This was in the midst of the dot-com boom. But, in their words, they weren't exactly a VC-funded, party-throwing, foosball-in-the-lobby-playing, free-beer-drinking outfit. (Unless it was other people's free beer.)

In 2002 Google bought the company. Now they are a small (but slightly bigger than before) team in Google focusing on helping people have their own voice on the web and organizing the world's information from the personal perspective.

In five minutes you can launch your own blog and you can't beat the price: free. If you want to accept ads from Google, you can even make money on your blog.

Please visit my blog at newclientmarketing.blogspot.com. You will find lots of ideas on how to woo and win clients. And you can respond to my posts with your comments.

Want more help finding all the clients you need? Here are two easy ways:

- You can attend our $25 Lunch and Learn seminar on: "How to Win Clients and Influence Referrals for Consultants" in San Diego on December 13 and Irvine on December 20. To reserve a spot call Henry DeVries, 800-514-4467 or e-mail henry@newclientmarketing.com.

CHAPTER 47: GET PUBLICITY

You must continually get the name of the firm out to the media. Research shows that publicity is the number one reason prospective clients will visit your Web site, so each piece of publicity should be designed to promote the Web site address.

You do not need psychic powers to predict the news. Certain stories appear with regularity. Sex, money and health are the three topics that are always in style. If you can provide new information on these subjects, the media will always welcome your input.

Other topics come in and out of style. Just like there are fashions in clothes and cars, there are fashions in news. To be a quoted authority, think not only news topic but also what is in style for this news season. Here is a month-by-month list of news topics. Newspapers, magazines, television, and radio are looking for fresh spins on these ageless news pegs.

- January   Fitness, prediction, Super Bowl

- February   Romance

- March   Spring training

- April   Baseball

- May   Moms

- June   Weddings, graduations, dads

- July   Vacations, Fourth of July

- August   Hot weather

- September   Back to school, football

- October   World Series, Halloween

- November   Elections, Thanksgiving

- December   Holidays, year-end wrap-ups

Another predictable aspect of media coverage is the anniversary story. For example, major news events are re-examined after intervals of one, ten, twenty, twenty-five and thirty years. Not only does history repeat itself, so does the news.

Ten Commandments of Media Relations

Top ten lists are fun. Here are the Ten Commandments of Media Relations, used by permission from a great new book on public relations by Richard Laermer and Michael Prichinello called *Full Frontal PR: Getting People Talking About You, Your Business, or Your Product.*

1. Thou shalt not bribe journalists. If your story isn't good enough for the media, or if your pitch isn't hitting home, regroup, fix the problem, and patch all the holes. Bribing a journalist is buying your way into the publication, and if that's what you want, make life easier for both of you and buy an advertisement. The best way to get a journalist to take your story is to prepare and hone the pitch so it delivers your message and addresses the media's real needs.

2. If you're happy with the way a story turns out, thou shalt not send a gift thanking the reporter. Your intentions may be perfectly honorable, but once again, a gift is problematic for a journalist. All you're doing is putting her ethics up for debate, because if she ever chooses to cover you in the future, a case can be made that you endeared your way in. Send a handwritten note expressing what a pleasure it was to work with her. That's best. It'll take longer to get there than a call or an e-mail, but it's the way to go. Also, if you decide to take a reporter out for dinner, discuss who pays for the meal beforehand. It's much simpler and more clear-cut for everyone.

3. Thou shalt strike the word *favor* from your media-relations vocabulary. You hear it day in and day out — PR and business people saying that they'll make a call because so-and-so at this paper owes them a favor. Eliminate the notion that the media owes you anything, and your expectations will be manageable.

4. Thou shalt not let your boss or colleagues tell you that they'll handle getting the media coverage if you're the one with the connections. You've gone to great pains to build the media relationship, so you should decide the best way to deal with someone. Friends in the media? Sure, that's a reality. But a friend, secondhand? Rarely, if ever. What your higher-up thinks is a friend usually is someone he talked to at a cocktail party.

5. Thou shalt not believe that whatever you're doing is too important to disclose. Entrepreneurs, inventors, and generic know-it-alls always seem to be in a very unhealthy form of "stealth mode," tediously toiling away on their next big idea in a locked lab guarded by nondisclosure agreements. But, of course, they want to be famous, too. The first thing to remember is that no matter

what you're doing, provided it isn't curing cancer or AIDS, someone else is doing something more important than you are.

6. Thou shalt not miss a deadline. Don't miss a deadline. Oh, and one more thing: Don't miss a deadline. The media live and die by the clock. If you're working with a reporter on your story, always make her schedule yours. If you're late with information, she's late with the story to her editor. This makes her look bad, and then the space in the paper or broadcast that was reserved for her story will have to be filled quickly, and then the whole production goes up in smoke.

7. Thou shalt not pitch one of your stories that just appeared in a competing newspaper or magazine and pretend you didn't see it or have anything to do with it. When that little fib comes back to haunt you — and it will — ouch, does that smart!

8. Thou shalt not break a deal. If you offer a reporter an exclusive, make sure it stays an exclusive. If you set up a press embargo for Friday, don't try to change the date to Monday or Tuesday later on. Success in PR is based on verbal agreements, so honor them, and there will be more deals for you to close in the future.

9. Thou shalt not lie. Never. Don't even exaggerate. This one doesn't need much explanation, other than to reiterate that lying about a product or service makes a journalist who reports it look like a dolt. Not to mention the obvious ethical problem on your end. Don't do it! But if it does happen, if you or someone in your company does lie, well then, call back, apologize, and make amends quickly. Say the devil made you do it, if you have to.

10. Thou shalt not give journalists only one option for using your story. If you are collaborating with a reporter on one angle, and it isn't working, don't just sigh and say, "Ah well, maybe next time." Find angles anew — there are always more. If you don't, you may as well just sit around and wait for the reporter to kill the piece and with it your opportunity for press coverage.

If you like these, the book has 17 more must-read commandments for anyone that wants to promote their professional service firm with PR.

Homework

Brainstorm ideas for press releases, events, and publicity that you could create and implement during the next year. Think of ways to tie in stories to predictable holidays and events. Come up with at least one idea per month, and then find a way to follow through.

Deliverable

A list of story or event ideas.

CHAPTER 48: SEND DIRECT MAIL

The best use of direct mail is to offer some form of free consultation or how-to literature. Your success will depend on testing various lists and offers until you find the one that clicks. Here are eight aspects to consider:

1. *What, me worry about the writing?* As we figure it, more than half of the success of your B2B offers depend on great strategic writing. Direct mail pioneer Ed Mayer is credited with coining the 40-40-20 rule. Simply put, 40 percent of your success will be determined by how well you define the audience (the list). Another 40 percent will be determined by how the audience responds to how it perceives your product, service and offer (writing the offer). Another 20 percent is determined by the creative package, which includes artwork and the copywriting (again writing).

2. *You're on my list.* Varying direct mail lists can change response rates from plus or minus 100 to 1,000 percent. (A favorite story of ours is about the upscale business that had an envelope come back stamped "cannot deliver without inmate registration number").

3. *Make me an offer.* In B2B direct mail it is crucial to have an offer that is quickly and easily understood. Offers are really a combination of the product and service, the price and payment terms, incentives and specific conditions.

4. *Permission granted.* With e-mail marketing you can benefit from a level of selling that is unavailable in the direct mail world. The key is the opt-in approach, in which prospects give their permission for you to contact them with offers. Here are 10 ways to leverage the power of e-mail:

5. *Build a permissible e-mail list* of prospects who would like to receive more information about your product or service.

6. *Diligently collect e-mail addresses* during all your lead-generating efforts, including trade shows and telemarketing.

7. *Embed links* to a merchandising Web site in your e-mails, giving you an instantaneous fulfillment package online.

8. *Avoid e-mail clutter by customizing.* By extracting specific information from your customer database, you have the ability to construct personalized messages for each reader.

Homework

Brainstorm the most cost-effective offers you could mail to prospects. Carefully evaluate the potential for ROI before committing to any one campaign. What can you offer? What lists will you buy? What is the potential value of a new customer procured this way? The cost?

CHAPTER 49: TRACK AND REFINE YOUR SYSTEM

If you want to see ROI, you'll need to track each lead generation program to refine your system. To quote the scientist Lord Kelvin, "If what you know cannot be measured your knowledge is of a meager and unsatisfactory kind."

For a seminar program, here is what you might want to track on a spreadsheet:

- Number of exposures to your message

- Responses generated

- Response rate

- Seminar attendees

- Attend rate

- Leads generated

- Number of Sales

- Sales volume

- Average sales

- One-time costs

- Implementation costs

- Cost per exposure

- Cost per response

- Cost per attendee

- Cost per lead

- Cost per sale

Homework

Assign a person to "own" your tracking system and give them the list above to build a spreadsheet or database that will track, in-house, the results of each of your lead generation efforts. Tailor the recordkeeping to your own business, of course. And commit to reviewing your ROI at least quarterly, making whatever course adjustments you think are necessary to raise ROI.

Deliverable

Assignment of tracking ownership

Database or spreadsheet

Scheduled reviews of ROI

CHAPTER 50: LEAD CONVERSION

The first 49 chapters focused on brand building and lead generation — the systems you must have in place before you can land clients.

We also believe that a strong lead conversion system is vital, and so we introduce concepts in this chapter that you may choose to pursue with fuller training and practice (we are graduates and advocates of Sandler Sales Training and highly recommend the book *You Can't Teach A Kid To Ride A Bike in A Seminar* by the late David Sandler).

The objective of doing what we recommend in this book is to get your phone to ring. What happens when the caller says they are interested in talking about hiring you? You need to arrange meetings with potential prospects. A meeting agreement is designed to set the ground rules for the meeting, and the ground rules are mutually agreed upon by both the marketer and the prospective client. In its most basic form, it's critical to determine the following before the meeting gets too far along:

- The time allotted for the meeting

- What each party's expectations for a successful meeting would be

- What will happen at the end of the meeting if there is a fit, or if there isn't a fit

Meeting agreements are an effective tactic for giving the marketer control of the lead conversion process, while permitting the prospective client to control the content. They help lower the prospect's fear of being sold something they don't want and are an excellent tool for building trust and rapport.

The meeting agreement is initiated by the marketer, who asks the prospect how much time can be allotted for the meeting, and what the prospect wants to accomplish. The marketer asks permission to ask questions so that he can be clear on what the prospect's needs are (translated, that means qualify the prospect). Further, the marketer states that if they get to the end of the meeting and there is not a fit between what the prospect wants and what the marketer can provide, that the prospect has permission to tell him "no." But if there is a fit, they should mutually determine what the next step should be.

Lead Conversion Action Plan

Every client is different; they have different pains, different businesses, different personalities.

The only way to master this lead conversion system is to practice it.

Start with a script to ask for an initial meeting. Work at it. Rehearse with somebody you trust. Get feedback. Go over your meeting agreement script until it's second nature; then work on making it sound spontaneous, personalized, and genuinely helpful. Don't worry if this doesn't come naturally to you at first; it's a whole new approach to closing sales.

At all times, remember that you're building trust. Is something you want to say likely to have the opposite effect? Make the prospect feel pressured or out of control?

Then don't say it.

The goal is to make your prospect feel as comfortable as possible discussing a potential business relationship. Don't pressure; seduce.

Appendix A: Further Reading

1001 Ways to Market Your Services—Even if You Hate to Sell by Rick Crandall (Contemporary Books, 1998, $16.95). This specific guide to marketing and sales methods provides 1001 real examples of professional marketing. It is filled with short, interesting examples, highlighted by pictures, tip boxes, and an "Action Agenda" at the end of each chapter with ideas and reminders to summarize.

Become a Recognized Authority In Your Field In 60 Days or Less! by Robert Bly (Alpha, 2002, $18.95). This book is about how to quickly become the preeminent, in-demand guru in your field and gives many steps on how to promote and market your knowledge and skills.

Creating New Clients—Marketing and Selling Professional Services by Kevin Walker, Cliff Ferguson, and Paul Denvir (Continuum, 2000, $31.95). This book outlines the skills required for maximum success in professional service firms, noting that selling themselves is based on chemistry, trust and an expected long-term business relationship. Their advice is based on the PACE Pipeline model, meaning that the opportunities for future business flow generated by accumulated efforts and activities.

Managing the Professional Service Firm by David Maister (Free Press Paperbacks, 1997, $25.00). In this general book on firm management, Maister states that all professional service firms have the same mission statement, essentially, "service, satisfaction, and success." His book gives advice on dealing with clients, management, partnerships and managing practices with multi-locations.

Marketing Your Consulting and Professional Services, 3rd Edition by Dick Connor and Jeff Davidson (John Wiley & Sons, 1997, $39.95). The book outlines four important "how-to's to ensure success:

- How to ensure satisfaction
- How to make client-centered marketing a natural activity
- How to make the most of your relationships
- How to work from your comfort zone

Million Dollar Consulting — The Professional's Guide to Growing a Practice by Alan Weiss (McGraw-Hill, 1998, $14.95). This guide urges the reader to push the envelope and go beyond their normal practices. It helps to target, land, and keep powerful clients, as well as establishes the firm's image and intensifies its profile. Weiss also gives tips on bases for fees and using new technology as a tool of business.

Rainmaking —The Professional's Guide to Attracting New Clients by Ford Harding (Adams Media Corp, 1994, $14.95). This is the self-help guide for a professional wanting to enhance his sales and marketing skills. It is divided into three parts: obtaining leads, advancing and closing the sale, and building the right marketing strategy for you. The book uses checklists and appendices to highlight the written and visual material, including how to develop and customize a marketing strategy, network effectively, write articles to draw clients, and use direct mail to attract new clients.

Marketing Plan Template

Worksheet 1: How To Improve Your Marketing in Five Steps

The first challenge for professionals and consultants is creating new clients. There is a proven process for marketing with integrity and getting a 400% to 2000% return on your marketing investment. To attract new clients, the best approach is the Educating Expert Model that demonstrates your expertise by giving away valuable information through writing and speaking. In addition, you can increase closing rates up to 50% to 100% by discovering and rehearsing the right questions to ask prospective clients.

The number one challenge for professionals and consultants is creating new clients. However, many professionals and consultants feel marketing is too time consuming, expensive or undignified. Even if they try a marketing or business development program, most professionals and consultants are frustrated by a lack of results. They even worry if marketing would ever work for them. And no wonder. According to a researcher from the Harvard Business School, the typical sales and marketing hype that works for retailers and manufacturers is not only a waste of time and money for professionals and consultants, it actually makes them less attractive to prospective clients (Maister, 1992, *Managing the Professional Service Firm*).

However, research has proven there is a better way. There is a proven process for marketing with integrity and getting an up to 400% to 2000% return on your marketing investment. At the New Client Marketing Institute we call it the Educating Expert Model, and the most successful professional service and consulting firms use it to get more clients than they can handle. The findings of our 8-year, $2 million research study about how the most successful professional and consulting firms use this model were published in our book, *Client Seduction* (Author House 2005).

To attract new clients, the best approach is to demonstrate your expertise by giving away valuable information through writing and speaking. Research shows independent professionals, management and technical consultants, corporate trainers, executive or personal coaches, marketing and creative firms, and HR and recruiting consultants can fill a pipeline with qualified prospects in as little as 30 days by offering advice to prospects on how to overcome their most pressing problems (DeVries and Bryson, 2005, *Client Seduction*).

Step One – How do you describe you?

As an elevator speech, please create one or two sentence answers for each

1. Who do you work with?

2. What problem do you solve?

3. Give examples of people you've helped

4. Results you get

Unfortunately, many professionals who learn the Educating Expert Model find the idea of writing and speaking too daunting and even mysterious. Most feel this is only for a select few, but that is a miscalculated view. In the beginning, it is not unusual to wonder how these other professionals and consultants get in front of audiences and get their how-to advice in print.

The good news is there exists a body of knowledge that some have discovered to grow their professional and consulting practices. As an example, management consulting firms like McKinsey & Co. pioneered the approach and have it down to a science (Bartlett, June 1996, "McKinsey & Co., *Harvard Business Review*). This is a growing trend. In 1991 a random survey of the top 1,000 U.S. law firms found that 89 percent held at least one client seminar per year. In 1999, 94 percent of law firms were regularly holding seminars. Lawyers at the top 1,000 firms ranked seminars as the most effective tool for cross-selling and gaining new clients (Source: FGI Research, 1999).

What should you do to increase revenues? First, understand that generating leads is an investment and should be measured like any other investment. Next, quit wasting money on ineffective means like brochures, advertising and sponsorships. The best marketing investment you can make is to get help creating informative Web sites, hosting persuasive seminars, booking speaking engagements, and getting published as a newsletter columnist and eventually book author.

Rather than creating a brochure, start by writing how-to articles. Those articles turn into speeches and seminars. Eventually, you gather the articles and publish a book through a strategy called print on demand self publishing (we've done it under 90 days and for less than a $1,000 for clients). Does it work? Here are a list of business best-seller titles by professionals and consultants that started out self-published (Source: *Southwest Airlines Spirit*, March 2005):

- *The One Minute Manager* by Kenneth Blanchard and Spencer Johnson: picked up by William Morrow & Co.

- *In Search of Excellence*, by Tom Peters (of McKinsey & Co.): in its first year, sold more than 25,000 copies directly to consumers — then Warner sold 10 million more.

- *Leadership Secrets of Attila the Hun*, by Weiss Roberts: sold half a million copies before being picked up by Warner.

Understanding the psychology of clients also provides critical evidence of the validity of the get published approach. Professional services and consulting are what economists sometimes call "credence" goods, in that purchasers must place great faith in those who sell the services (Bloom, October 1984, "Effective Marketing for Professional Services," *Harvard Business Review*). What does the research say about client choice, satisfaction and dissatisfaction of professionals and consultants? Here are the five ways prospects judge you (Aaker, 1995, *Strategic Market Management*) and my views of how the Educating Expert Model is the perfect fit:

1. **Competence**. Knowledge and skill of the professional or consultant and their ability to convey trust and confidence (you demonstrate and prove your expert knowledge by speaking and writing)

2. **Tangibles**. Appearance of physical facilities, communication materials, equipment and personnel (you do this by the appearance of your Web site, book and how-to handouts)

3. **Empathy**. Caring, individualized attention that a firm provides its clients (educating people to solve problems before they hire you proves you care)

4. **Responsiveness**. Willingness to help customers and provide prompt service (when you promise to give people things like special reports and white papers, do it promptly)

5. **Reliability**. Ability to perform the promised service dependably and accurately (prospective clients will judge you on how organized your seminars, speeches and Web site are)

Step Two – How do you rate yourself?

Please rate yourself on the following:

1. **Competence**. Knowledge and skill of the professional or consultant and their ability to convey trust and confidence

2. **Tangibles**. Appearance of physical facilities, communication materials, equipment and personnel

3. **Empathy**. Caring, individualized attention that a firm provides its clients

4. **Responsiveness**. Willingness to help customers and provide prompt service

5. **Reliability**. Ability to perform the promised service dependably and accurately Even if you believe in the Educating Expert Model, how do you find time to do it and still get client and admin work done? No professional or consultant ever believes they have too much time on their hands. Nothing worth happening in business ever just happens. The answer is to buy out the time for marketing. You need to be involved, but you should not do this all on your own. Trial and error is too expensive of a learning method. Wouldn't it be better if someone helped you who knows the tricks and shortcuts? We can show you how to leverage your time and get others to do most of the work for you, even if you are a solo practitioner.

Step Three – How would you summarize your business?

This will help you create a written one-page executive summary of your business. Please complete one sentence answers for each.

1. **Target**: We help…

2. **Pain**: Who struggle with…

3. **Predicament**: Which makes them…

4. **Answer**: What I do Is…

5. **Benefits**: So they can…

6. **Why me**: Unlike typical people in my field, my difference is…

How much should you invest in marketing? That depends on your business goals, but here are some norms. In terms of time, figure 25 to 50% of your time. In dollars, law firms generally spend about 2 percent of their gross revenues on marketing, and the average expenditure is about $136,000. Marketing costs for accounting firms average about 7 percent to 10 percent of gross revenue (Source: *The New*

York Times, November 15, 2001). The typical architecture, engineering, planning, and environmental consulting firm spent a record 5.3 percent of their net service revenue on marketing (Source: *ZweigWhite's 2003 Marketing Survey of A/E/P & Environmental Consulting Firms*).

Here are some of the key benefits of following the Educating Expert Model:

- Allows your message to be heard above the noise of all the other professionals and consultants

- Systematizes your marketing with a proactive, monthly approach that is simple and affordable to implement

- Makes it easier for your clients and business advocates to refer potential clients to you

- Creates multiple streams of income because prospects actually pay for you to market to them

- Increases closing rates up to 50% to 100% by discovering and rehearsing the right questions to ask prospective clients

- Produces all-help, no-hype marketing you actually feel proud to communicate

- Quits wasting money on ineffective tactics like brochures, sponsorships and cold-calling

- Leverages your time so you get more results in less time

The New Client Marketing Institute works with independent professionals, management and technical consultants, corporate trainers, executive or personal coaches, marketing and creative firms, and HR and recruiting consultants who are struggling to attract enough clients. We have a 15-year track record of measurably improving revenues for professional service firms and service businesses. Through one-on-one brainstorming, small group practice sessions and in-house marketing retreats we share more than 1,000 pragmatic strategies and tactics.

We've had very good results guiding our clients to increase revenues through more new clients, more fee income per client and more money from past clients. Here are just a few concrete examples:

- Through an informational Web site and electronic newsletter we helped create, one management consultant client added an additional $100,000 in revenue from speaking engagements and sales of information products within 2 years

- In 45 days one client who is a consultant to the home building industry was able to launch a Web site and education expert campaign that helped him double his business in a year

- Using one strategy alone a Web marketing consultant client was able to double his income and add $100,000 of revenue in one year through just one strategy

- By switching over to the model, a marketing services client was able to receive a 2000% return on investment its new marketing campaign that featured how-to advice seminars and articles form senior executives

- When an IT consulting company gave up cold calling and switched to our model, the quality of their leads dramatically improved and closed deals quickly increased by 25%

- Using these strategies of seminars and getting published, a law firm client has grown in a few years from a regional practice to a national firm

- A well established regional accounting firm client reported they were able to accomplish more in 6 months with our methods than they had in three years on their own

- An advertising agency used the strategy to double revenues from $4.5 to $9.6 million in five years and earn a spot in the *Ad Age* 500

- With the model, a 100-year-old financial services firm was able to double awareness and create 100,000 qualified leads per year for its advisors

Step Four – What specific results have you achieved for clients?

Use percentages, numbers and time. What client stories can you tell to illustrate results you obtain?

Step Five – How will you promote your business?

Please complete one sentence answers for each.

1. **Small-scale seminar strategy**

2. **Speaking strategy**

3. **Get published strategy**

4. **E-zine strategy**

5. **Networking strategy**

6. **Referral strategy**

Worksheet 2: Your Perfect Niche Market

Who are your three top target markets? Fill them into the following grid, then answer "Yes" or "No" to each "Ideal Target Qualifler." This grid can help you to prioritize which market to target FIRST — and you may need to shape your message specifically for each target market.

1. Do they have problems you can solve?

2. Do they know they have a problem?

3. Are they willing and able to solve the problem?

4. Are there a lot of them?

5. Is there enough room in your space to be competitive?

6. Can you buy lists to help you reach them?

7. Have you already established credibility with businesses like them?

8. Do their issues interest you?

9. Are they geographically desirable?

10. Will they make good references?

Their Pains

Next, consider your perfect market. What are the pains they have that you solve?

Pain

My prospects are frustrated about...

Worried about.....

Concerned that.....

Worksheet 3: Your Marketing DNA

The Promise: First Draft

Rosser Reeves, the author of the phrase, "unique selling proposition," or USP, says you need a unique message about you versus the competition.If you cannot concisely describe the uniqueness of your idea (and create some excitement in potential users), you may not have the basis for a successful business.

There are several questions to ask about your business to determine a USP:

What is unique about your business or brand vs. direct competitors? Brainstorm for 5 minutes.

_____

_____

_____

_____

You probably found a whole list of things that set you apart; the next questions will help you decide which of these to focus on.

- Which of these factors are most important to the buyers and end users of your business or brand?

- Which of these factors are not easily imitated by competitors?

- Which of these factors can be easily communicated and understood by buyers or end users?

Next, you'll construct a memorable message (USP) of these unique, meaningful qualities about your business or brand.

USE MEANINGFUL, REAL, CONCRETE WORDS with REAL, CONCRETE MEANINGS.

No doublespeak or Dilbert-speak (i.e., nobody understands "solutions," let alone finds it memorable)

Geoffrey Moore, in Crossing the Chasm, uses the following tool to craft differentiation statements for service firms (especially high-tech). See what you can do filling in the blanks for your organization.

For (target customer)_____

Who (statement of the need or opportunity)_____

_____.

(product or service name) _____is a

(product category) _____

That (key benefit / compelling reason to buy)_____

Unlike (primary competitive alternative) _____

Our product (statement of primary differentiation) _____

Mark LeBlanc in Growing Your Business! suggests a simple, Conversational (not marketing-speak) answer to a simple question: **What do you do?**

I/We work with (target customer)_____

Who WANT (3-5 word outcome) _____

and (3-5 word outcome) _____

Example: We work with people who want to start a business and small business owners who want to grow their business.

Marketing DNA Assessment

Educating Expert Model

Before you can begin attracting clients, you need to create a marketing genetic code that is attractive to clients. All of your marketing messages, from networking discussions to speeches, will contain the elements of this marketing DNA. Here are 10 steps that will help you create these all-important marketing genes.

---

1. Create a business name or a Web site name that gives potential clients a hint at the results you can produce for them. The worst possible name or Web site name is your name. Sorry to say, clients don't want us, they want results.

2. Write a headline for your Web site and marketing materials that describes your audience and the results you produce for them. Do this in no more than 10 words. Mine is "We help professionals and consultants attract all they clients they need."

3. Name your client's pain. What are your client's worries, frustrations and concerns that you help solve? This is also called the FUD factor: fear, uncertainty and doubt.

4. Describe your solution or methodology for solving these pains. What process do you follow to produce results? Offering a proprietary problem-solving process that you name and trademark is best. This answers the all-important question in their minds: "Why should I do business with you instead of one of your competitors?"

5. State the common misperception that holds many back from getting results. Why doesn't everybody do what you named in step 4?

6. Tell your clients what they need to do in general to solve their problem. Pretend they weren't hiring you and you had to describe the steps they should take for success.

7. List any other benefits they get from following your methods. What other good things do people get when they do what you advise?

8. Elaborate on your track record of providing measurable results for clients. Be specific as much as possible. Use numbers, percentages and time factors.

9. Create a Web site with free tips articles on how to solve these pains. Each article should be about 300 to 600 words. What's a good format? Consider the numbered tips approach you are reading right now (easy to write, easy to read).

10. Make prospects an offer of a free special report on your Web site. You are offering to trade them a valuable piece of information for their e-mail address. Tell them they will also receive a tips e-newsletter from you. Assure them you will maintain their privacy and they can easily opt off your list any time they want.

Genetic Code Exercise

Genetic Element	Your Wording	Score (from −10 to +10 points)
1. Name of your business (result name is best, just your name is worst)		
2. Audience + result headline (11 words or less is best)		
3. Name their pain: worries, frustration, concerns (a syndrome is best)		
4. Your solution including model or methodology, (proprietary process is best)		
5. The common misperception that holds many back from getting results		
6. What they need to do in general to solve their problem that you are an expert in		
7. Other benefits they get by following your methods		
8. Your track record of providing measurable results		
9. Web site with free resources		
10. Trade e-mail address for e-zine list for free special report		
	TOTAL (out of 100)	

WORKSHEET 4

Your Pain Survey

To get people to attend your seminar, you should offer proprietary research you regularly undertake with your target market. Some of this can be secondary studies (other people's research you find in textbooks, journals, magazines and the Internet) and some can be primary (actual interviews you conduct). Here's how to create an interview questionnaire.

Section 1: Their Demographics. Who's answering? Do They Fit Your Target Market Profile? Don't go hog-wild; this isn't about them as individuals. It's about you and what you need to know.

Job Title: _____

Industry: _____

\# of Employees:

Section 2: Their Pains. We're trying to find out what they believe and what they're ready to act on, so we can know what to offer folks like them. The first two questions are open-ended, consisting of our BEST GUESSES about what they're frustrated, worried, or concerned about.

During the next 12 months, would you say the following are high, medium, or low priorities for you and your company?

Section 3. Do you agree or disagree with each of the following statements?

Here we try to get at the ASSUMPTIONS and BELIEFS that underlie their reasons for buying — or not. What might they believe that would incline them to act faster, or slower? To buy your offerings or not to? Try to phrase these possible beliefs in a *non-leading* way. Again, a couple old "truisms' never hurt.

Statement	Agree	Neither Agree nor Disagree	Disagree

Section 3: The Big Kahuna: The Open-Ended, Heart's-Desire, No-Holds-Barred, Bleeding-Pain question.

If you were an all-powerful being and you could improve three things about your sales force and sales process, what three things would you choose?

a.

b.

c.

Worksheet 5: Your Proprietary Process Steps

The Process

You already have a process. It's the way you do things, step by step, from the minute a client engages with you until the work is done. You're going to outline it now. Only one constraint: At this stage, don't aim for more than 10 steps. Keep it short and simple. And if you only end up with four steps or five, you're fine, too.

Step 1: We _____

_____

Step 2: We _____

_____

Step 3: We _____

_____

Step 4: We _____

_____

Step 5: We _____

_____

Step 6: We _____

_____

Step 7: We _____

_____

Step 8: We _____

_____

Step 9: We _____

_____

Step 10: We _____

_____

The Process Name

We think a simple formula will name your process 90% of the time. It's a "Mad Lib" approach.

The _____   _____

System / Process.

Use the space below to come up with words that describe what you do and how. Some combination of them may be your best process name.

Worksheet 6: Demonstrating Expertise

Free Information

One of our mantras is "Free Resources." You need to demonstrate your competence by writing and giving away information that proves you know your stuff. Most people, we know, hate writing and avoid it like you know what. But you've got to have good content for everything else in your lead generation system, and you'll need a good few solid topics to get you going. These topics, or headlines, will become the basis for your seminars, your articles, your columns, your speeches — everything you do.

To generate a lot of ideas fast, go back to your Pain worksheet. How can you fill in the blanks in the spaces below to make a gripping headline for a prospect that's focused like a laser beam on his or her frustrations, worries, and concerns? (If you start looking at magazine covers, you'll recognize these "recipes." They're everywhere.) Thanks to Joan Stewart at the Publicity Hound for some of these headlines (For more free publicity for your professional services business, sign up for "The Publicity Hound's Tips of the Week," an electronic newsletter. Subscribe at www.PublicityHound.com and receive by autoresponder the handy list "89 Reasons to Send a News Release.")

Put a star next to ten or fifteen headlines that really appeal to you; then go back and fill in the blanks.

A Quiz: Test Your _____ Smarts

Cash in on _____Trends

Chasing the Right_____

Cool Tools for _____

Common Errors That Kill _____

Part-Time Tactics for Full-Time _____

Discover the 7 Essential Elements That Guarantee_____

Finding the_____That is Uniquely You

Good News For / About_____

How to Bounce Back from _____

How to Get Other People to _____

How to Handle _____

How to Make_____ Work for You

How to Turn _____ into _____

Mastering the Art of _____

No More _____

Questions and Answers About_____

Straight Talk from a _____

The Great_____ Dilemma

The Most Beginner-Friendly _____

The Last Word on _____

The Amazing Solution for _____

The Best and Worst Ideas for_____

The Complete Guide to _____

The Worst Mistakes You Can Make When _____

Top 10 _____Dos and Don'ts

What's HOT and NOT in_____

When Not to _____

Your Must-Know Guide to _____

_____with Pizzazz!

_____and Grow Rich

_____ on the Cheap

5 Ways to Get More from Your _____

5 No-Fail Strategies for_____

6 Secrets to Successful_____

7 Ways to Keep Your_____ Dreams Alive

7 Ways to Avoid the Most Deadly_____ Mistakes

8 Ways to Avoid the Worst_____ Mistakes

9 Formulas for Fantastic _____

10 User-Friendly Facts for _____

10 Tips to Jump-start Your_____

11 Questions You Must Ask When You're _____ _____

12 Tactics to Open Up_____

13 Tips That Will Make a _____ Smile

10 Time-Tested Tips for Becoming a _____

25 Quick _____Tips to Use Now

Worksheet 7

How To Turn Seminars Into Increased Revenue

Generating new client leads through seminars is a proven strategy. But some professional service firms and technology service companies are frustrated with a lack of turnout for the seminars they host. By following some best-practice strategies, you can dramatically increase seminar and event attendance.

First, scrutinize your proposed topic by asking yourself some hard questions. If prospective clients attend this seminar, what beneficial information will they receive? Is this information that my competition either cannot, or does not, offer? Is this information a strong enough pull to justify them spending their precious time with us?

Next, examine how you spread the word. Do you have the right mailing list? If so, maybe direct mail alone is not enough to deliver enough prospects to your next seminar. A key to attracting high-level executives is to reinforce direct mail messages with phone calls. These calls also can provide valuable feedback on how prospects view the seminar topic and subject matter.

Perhaps time and distance are keeping you apart. If you serve clients that are located throughout the country (or perhaps, the world), there is an online alternative to face-to-face seminars.

An online seminar (or Webinar) is an interactive, real-time way to hold online meetings and conferences. By eliminating the barriers of time and space, Webinars enable you to share information with thousands of customers or partners anywhere in the world, through a standard Web browser. With a Webinar you can conduct seminars, training, product demonstrations and collaborative meetings, thereby significantly lowering the cost of communications and reaching people whom otherwise would not participate because they are unable to travel to your meeting.

Let-it-flow-chart

It's one thing to have a great idea for an event to attract potential clients. But it's quite another to pull it off successfully. The myriad of small details involved can make or break an event. Here are some recommendations to maximize the success of your next lead generation seminar.

1. Develop a checklist and timeline for pre/post seminar activities

2. Decide if this will be a free briefing or an event that you will charge for (there is a time and place for both)

3. Use informal research to pre-test topics to make sure the one you choose has the most appeal to your target audience

4. Make sure the letters or invitations you use reflect a first-class image for your firm

5. Confirm registrations 48 hours before the event by e-mail

6. Deliver seminar content that is of real value to clients, not a thinly disguised sales pitch for your services

7. After the seminar, make it easy for the potential client to contact you in the future by sending a thank you e-mail/letter with phone number and Web address

8. Conduct an organized follow up five to ten days after the seminar or event in an effort to start a dialogue with potential clients

9. Measure how much the seminars cost and how much revenue was ultimately generated to calculate your return on investment (ROI)

Getting the word out

Event letters or invitations should be mailed or e-mailed approximately four weeks prior to the event. Give registrants the option to call the 800 number, fax, e-mail or utilize the on-line event registration application on the Internet to register for an event. When possible, it is helpful to provide detailed information on your invitations for the location of your event and an overview of what will be covered. Here are some business-to-business seminar scheduling guidelines:

- No seminars on weekends

- Avoid Monday and Friday

- Avoid seminars in a holiday week (Fourth of July)

- Check for conflicting industry events

- The best months to hold a seminar in rank order are:

  1. March

  2. October

  3. April

  4. September

  5. November

  6. January

7. February

8. June

9. May

10. July

11. August

12. December

Telemarketing calls can increase registrations five percent beyond the registration rate from direct mail. Calling is conducted one to three weeks prior to the event. Many seminar experts recommend three calls attempts per contact with voice messages on the first and third attempts.

Typically, only 50 percent of those who say they will attend a free seminar actually attend. To minimize no-shows, confirmation e-mails are another option to consider. Send an e-mail confirmation 48 hours prior to the event. The e-mail confirmation will act as a reminder of the event and provide them date, time, location and directions. E-mail confirmations can greatly increase the attendance rate at the event.

Final thoughts on details

You might ask yourself, are all these details that important?

Remember, the purpose of seminars is to introduce you to potential clients and provide evidence on what it would be like to do business with you. Clients will form many preliminary impressions about you through the seminars. Know this: you are being judged on if you are organized, thorough and willing to invest in the relationship by providing valuable information.

Worksheet 8: Referrals and Networking

The *A B C's* of A Strong Referral Program

For this exercise, you'll need to break your Rolodex down into four groups.

A's are the people who love you, and whom you love. Aim for 25. You'll reach out and touch them on a monthly basis, give them something fun or creative or useful, and reinforce how important they are to you. You'll also tell them that you would welcome their referrals.

B's are your next 75 biggest fans. You'd LIKE them to become A's…people who sing your praises and send you business. You'll reach them bimonthly.

C's are the remainder of your list who may some day refer business your way, or do more business with you. You'll send them something four times per year.

(If there are folks remaining in your Rolodex who, for whatever reason, will never be a referral source, simply don't assign them a letter at all. They become "Everybody Else.")

MAIL: By the _____ day of each month. Pencil in ideas of what to send.

Networking Goals

This one's easy. Your goal: To build your permission e-mail mailing list by meeting people and asking for their cards, routinely. You should set a goal to achieve each month and do everything you can to live up to it.

GOAL:

Number of cards per month to enter into e-mail list: _____

Number of events to attend per month: _____

ORGANIZATIONS TO CHECK OUT/JOIN:

_____

_____

_____

_____

_____

_____

Worksheet 9: Pulling the Plan Together

E-zine Plan

An e-zine or e-newsletter that hits your prospects is priceless in terms of keeping your name in front of people. Every newsletter needs two things: Solid content, and an offer/call to action.

Use the following grid to plan your e-newsletter strategy for the next year. If you need ideas for content, go back to the titles you generated in worksheet 6.

...And Bribery

What can you afford to offer as a fun, "quick responder" contest item to keep people interested when they see your name in the Inbox? Offering a fun, interesting promotional item is a great way to keep "Unsubscribe" rates low.

_____

_____

_____

_____

_____

_____

_____

_____

_____

_____

_____

_____

_____

_____

_____

_____

A Warm-Calling Script for Invitation Followup

Hello, Mr./Ms./Dr. _____, my name is _____

_____. **Is this a bad time to talk?**

I'm calling from _____. We work with _____

_____ who want _____, _____

_____, and _____.

The reason I'm calling is that I sent you an invitation to a seminar/webinar about ___
_____ a few days back. The event is going to cover proprietary
research we've performed on _____ and will help
you to understand how you compare to other companies like yours.
I'm calling to find out whether you'll be able to join us for the briefing, and "No" is a
fine answer.

Can I put you down as an attendee for that day?

The real secret of success is activity. Thirty minutes a day is all we ask. Copy this down and post it around your office, your house, your car. Take it to heart. It's the key to making your program a success.

The Universe Rewards Activity

You need to have a system to follow, or things just won't get done. Your system will look slightly different from everybody else's when you're finished with it, because you're going to choose to do certain activities and wait to implement others based on your unique business, your needs, your resources (time, people, and money) and your target audience.

The following is a sample plan, taken straight from the real world.

Every Month: Activities we must do
· Mail seminar invitations

· Telemarket seminar

· Hold seminar

· Mail teleseminar invitations

· Telemarket teleseminar

· Hold teleseminar

· Write syndicated column

· Distribute syndicated column

· Send bi-monthly e-newsletters

· Send drip sales letters

· Mail to 25 referrals (A, B, and/or C)

· Mail to 25 target speaking groups

· Attend 4 networking events to gather business cards

· Test, track and tune results

Review all the previous worksheets and write down what needs to be done to make this happen. What activities must be handled? Who will be responsible for doing them?

Your Must-Do Activities Every Month

#	What?	Who?
1		
2		
3		
4		
5		
6		
7		
8		
9		
10		
11		
12		
13		
14		
15		
16		
17		
18		
19		
20		
21		
22		
23		
24		
25		
26		
27		

About The Author

Henry DeVries, MBA is a leading marketing expert for marketing services providers. His pragmatic and entertaining presentations have had a positive impact on thousands of marketing communications consultants at advertising agencies, public relations firms, interactive Internet/Web companies, and graphic design studios. In his writing, speaking and mentoring he reveals more than 1,000 pragmatic strategies to achieve marketing returns of 400% to 2000%. Career highlights include:

- Marketing faculty member at UC San Diego Extension since 1984

- Speaker, workshop leader, facilitator and coach

- Author of *Self-Marketing Secrets, Client Seduction* and *Pain Killer Marketing*

- Former president of an *Ad Age* 500 advertising and public relations agency

- Founder of New Client Marketing Institute, marketing training and research company

- Completed specialized training at Harvard Business School

- Clients have appeared on Oprah, Larry King, David Letterman and in *U.S. News & World Report, Glamour, Good Housekeeping, The New York Times, The Los Angeles Times, Wall Street Journal, Glamour,* and the Associated Press

Marketing, Motivation and Humor Topics

- **Self-Marketing Secrets** – How to Promote You, Your Company and Your Ideas

- **Beyond Clientology 101** – How To Win Clients And Influence Referrals By Turning Expertise Into Leads

- **Help and Grow Rich Motivation** – Get A Dozen Things You Want By Helping Others Get What They Want

- **Don't Join Any Club That Would Have You As A Member** – Ways to Build Your Nation of Relationships

- **Pleased to Media You** – A Humorous Look at Becoming a Quoted Authority Online and Offline

- **Why Friends Come and Go But Enemies Accumulate** – Nine Leadership Lessons for Your Workplace

Henry can be reached at henry@newclientmarketing.com or at 800-514-4467.